COME ALIVE

OVERCOME CHALLENGES – LIVE YOUR PURPOSE

UNLEASH THE REAL YOU

DAVID GIBSON JR

ISBN: 978-0-578-49702-0

DEDICATION

This book is dedicated to Ross Givens,
who helped me gain a new understanding of
why we all must COME ALIVE.

CONTENTS

A GREATER VERSION OF YOU IS EMERGING...

INTRODUCTION

IT TAKES COURAGE TO RISE ABOVE FEAR, AND AS UNCOMFORTABLE AS IT MAY BE, ONE MUST NEVER FORGET THAT ON THE OTHER SIDE OF FEAR IS FREEDOM

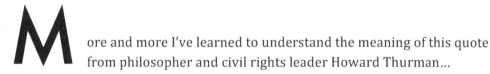 ore and more I've learned to understand the meaning of this quote from philosopher and civil rights leader Howard Thurman...

"Don't ask yourself what the world needs. Ask yourself what makes you come alive, and go do that, because what the world needs is people who have come alive."

It's a statement that really makes you think—What makes me come alive? What is it that brings me life, pure joy, and deep satisfaction?

At some point we each will find ourselves searching to discover the meaning of life, but I believe there's more that we're seeking. As much as we aim to find the meaning of life, we also deep down are searching for the experience of being alive.

Let's be clear, there's a huge difference between existing and being alive. You started existing when you were a fetus in your mother's womb. You come alive when you start becoming everything that you were created to be. When you evolve into the complete person you were intended to be—operating with clarity, purpose, and focus.

Ask enough people and you'll discover that we all want to be happy. We each want to be filled with joy and satisfied with our life's experience. We want to love who we are, what we do, and how we do it. We want to know that we matter and that we're special. We all have a desire to live abundant and purposeful lives.

What's the point of being alive if you don't at least try to do something remarkable?

The fact is that regardless of what your life currently looks like or no matter what your life experience has been like up until this point...never lose sense that you ARE capable of doing something remarkable. *How do I know?* Because you're capable of coming alive, and doing remarkable things is a byproduct of you evolving into the complete person you were intended to be.

...But the reality is that not everyone taps into their full potential and experiences what it's like to come alive. As the well-known saying goes, *"Everybody dies but not everybody lives"*.

We all have the capacity to grow, to improve, and to evolve into our greater selves, but many people don't. We each could do more, experience more, and become more, but many never do. There are desires, dreams, and visions within us all but the reality is that many neglect to pursue these impulses.

Why not? That's the "million-dollar" question...why is it that many sit on their gifts and never pursue their passions? Why is it that most people live their fears instead of living their dreams? Why do so many people settle and accept things in their life that were never meant to be? —Finding themselves imprisoned by their comfort zone, their fears, or maybe even their past. Born an eagle capable of flying and soaring to new heights in life, but trapped in a cage that's designed for a parrot. Every time they attempt to spread their wings...they are limited by this prison, which hinders them from experiencing all that they were intended to experience.

Maybe you can relate as you're reading this—you know that there's more life you can experience and that there's greater within you, but it seems like you're stuck. It seems like you're trapped. It seems like your life has been limited. You've lost the belief in yourself. Your fear of failure has weighed more than your desire for success. Your past has you pinned down and you feel like you can't escape it. There's a voice in your head that says you can't do it and a part of you believes it.

You feel like that eagle trapped in a cage that's designed for a parrot.

I wrote this book to help you realize that you don't have to live in a cage. My mission is to help you fly and achieve more. It's my goal to help you come alive and experience your abundant life.

I know that feeling of being *"trapped"* and *"stuck"* and in the chapters that follow I will share with you how I was able to overcome these feelings and step out of the cage. This book consists of a few insights that have benefitted me as I take this never-ending journey of becoming the best version of myself.

Perception is reality, so if you want a different reality then you have to change your perception. If you want a greater reality then you have to establish a greater perception of who you are, what you're capable of achieving, and what's available in the world around you.

By the end of this book you'll understand how to do just that. Let today be the last day of the way you used to be and the first day of the rest of your life. It's time to **COME ALIVE.**

WHO ARE YOU?

YOU CAN'T REACH WHAT'S IN FRONT OF YOU UNTIL YOU FIRST LET GO OF WHAT'S BEHIND YOU

Your life will change the moment you decide you're going to be who you were created to be. Making this decision means that you have to know who you are. Self-awareness is the first step to self-empowerment. To be empowered you have to separate your truth from what's false. This is what gives birth to freedom—from your past, your insecurities, and the opinions of others. In this chapter, you'll discover how changing your story and becoming the real you can transform your life as you know it.

TELL ME WHO YOU ARE

He shook my hand, gripped it firmly, and looked me directly in my eye and asked me..."*Who are you?*"

"*My name is David Gibson.*"

"*No, I got your name...but who are you!?*"

The man I was being introduced to was an old time friend of my grandfather's. I never had the opportunity to meet my grandfather, he passed before I was even born, but I'd heard countless stories about the type of man he was—firm, direct, and no-non-sense. His friend who stood before me shared the same firm personality.

He spoke in a tone that was sharp and with a voice that demanded your attention—very similar to Morgan Freeman as Mr. Clark in the movie *Lean On Me*.

With an irritated and impatient look on his face, he stood in front of me awaiting my response. After already telling him my name, I was confused to what answer he was looking for.

"I'm going to ask you one more time and it'll be the last time I ask you son, 'ya hear?! WHO ARE YOU?"

I had to come up with my answer quick..."*I am...*"

He interrupted me before I could even put a thought to what I would say and said..."SOMEBODY! I...AM...SOMEBODY! Let me hear you say it!"

Confused, I repeated after him, *"I...am...somebody?"*

"Say it like you mean it!"

"I AM SOMEBODY!"

He shook my hand, smiled, and said..."*and don't let anybody tell you otherwise! You get to decide who you are and when you realize that your life will never be the same."*

I AM....

"I am..." is the beginning of a statement. It's made up of two simple words, but what you place after those two words will serve as a declaration. What you put after them will shape your reality. Whether you realize it or not, you are the author of your story and you create the narrative in your head.

Regardless of what life has tried to convince you, you are somebody. You are and were born enough. You don't need to prove anything, do anything, or be anything more than who you are. In order to come alive and create a life that you don't want to escape, you must begin to identify with the real you and operate in your uniqueness.

IDENTITY

Your identity has to do with who you think you are and how you perceive yourself. It's the role you choose to play in life. It's a narrative that you create in your mind, which becomes your own personal story. We each live in our own story. Our story is what controls our view on life. It's important that you are driven by a story that makes you come alive. Why? *Your story directly influences how effective you are at your strategies for success.* You can have all the tried and true strategies, but if you don't have the right attitude, because of a self-sabotaging story, you'll miss the mark of achievement.

It's your responsibility to form, shape, and live out your own identity and create your own story. Not doing so, allows something or someone else to do so. Your fears, your past, and the opinions of other people can leave you forming an inaccurate perception of who you really are, causing you to live a life that's not an accurate display of the person you truly can become. It's unfortunate, but many people fall into this category. They spend their entire lives being something that they're not—allowing their insecurities to dictate their decisions, doubt to paralyze their potential, and their past to control their future. Even worse, they end up settling in life because they accept the image placed on them by other people. *You can't reach your greatest potential when you're living with a false identity.*

Your identity is not defined by the lowest points in your life. Your struggle doesn't have to become your identity. What someone did or what happened in your life doesn't have to change how you view and perceive yourself. Your future doesn't have to be your past. Where you've come from doesn't have to be where you stay. Someone else's opinion of you doesn't have to be your truth. You have the authority to define who you are and what you believe about yourself—you are not a failure, you are not a mistake, you are not a lost cause. You are special. You are unique. You are fearfully and wonderfully made and created for something amazing. Life will never be different until you first see it differently.

You change your world by changing your story. Despite what may have occurred in your life, you have to believe that you belong at the table of greatness and that you are destined to do great things.

To come alive you have to decide who you're going to be based on the truth about what's in you. This means aligning everything about you with your true identity and not making the mistake of conforming to the world around you.

We are not products of our circumstances, we are products of our decisions. Though changing your self-perception can be difficult, you can make the decision on how you choose to view yourself. For example, if you've always struggled in school as a student then it may be difficult to believe that you could somehow write a best selling book one day. Or, if you've grown accustomed to living in poverty it could be hard to believe that you could one day be a millionaire. Why is that? Because it's easier to remember the past than it is to see the possibilities of the future. How you identified yourself in the past can become a hard to escape prison. However, the path to redemption from your past is not to run from it, but to try to understand it and use it as a foundation for growth. Socrates said, *"The secret to change is to focus all of your energy not on fighting the old, but on building the new."* You have to change the meaning you give your past and how you choose to interpret it. As you evolve from your experience, you can reinvent your identity.

Notice how I mentioned the ability you have to *"reinvent your identity"*. People often say that they haven't found themselves...but the self is not something you find, it's something you create. You reinvent yourself as you discover new facets of about yourself and as the world changes. No matter how challenging life gets, your identity is never lost. It's always present. It doesn't get found or discovered...it emerges. It's created. You are not defined by your circumstances. They reveal who you are, but only if you become clear on your identity. Otherwise you'll find yourself conforming to your circumstances and accepting things to be normal that were never meant to be.

Feeling hopeless, feeling powerless, or being miserable...life doesn't have to be this way. In fact, it's not supposed to be. You were created for more and you deserve more out of life. You need to experience a rebirth. The old you may be anxious, insecure, and depressed, but the real you is bold, wise, adventurous, and full of love and power. To acquire more life you have to be willing to sacrifice the old you and become the real you. This is a pivotal decision in creating a bigger future than the present you are living.

THE REAL YOU

The real you is born when you eliminate your preconceived notions and allow the truth to live through you. True identity is formed through self-awareness and by letting go of conditioned thoughts and beliefs. It's important to discover new things about yourself, but it's also important to unlearn things that are stopping you from reaching new levels in your life. You have to clear your mind of negative views of who you think you are and learn to see yourself differently. You make room for new experiences by emptying out the long held and outdated limiting beliefs that have been halting your success. It's not who you are that's holding you back, it's who you think you're not. You can't allow those insecure voices in your head and the voices of your past to make you feel unworthy of success. Your mind may be full of ideas, thinking patterns, and destructive emotions that no longer serve you. You have to eliminate them. Sing a new song, flip the script, change the narrative, and look at yourself through the lens of truth. You have to make it a point to be in alignment with the real you in order to avoid living an unauthentic life.

You are gifted, you are talented, and you deserve to live a life of success. There is only one you. Don't devalue yourself. Don't diminish your worth. You deserve to be happy, healthy, wealthy, and prosperous. You are full of life, power, and abundance, and you have the ability within you to be unstoppable. You can achieve whatever you set your mind to. As you discard the old identities and expired reputations, a metamorphosis into the new you can occur.

However, emerging into the real you isn't always easy. Venturing beyond who you've always thought you were and becoming who you desire to be will stretch you in many ways. Your true identity will only be found outside of your comfort zone, but this is a journey that you have to take to come alive. In order to open up your mind to the exciting world of possibilities, you have to break the rules of your current reality and your historical thoughts.

CHANGE YOUR STORY

They say the hardest prison to escape is your mind. I spent a part of my life trapped in this prison. I grew up intimidated to speak to others and had a fear of expressing myself. I never really felt like I mattered and doubted that there was anything significant that I had to offer. This narrative repeated itself over and over again until it became my story. This affected every area of my life—from how I viewed myself, to how I interacted with other people, to how I performed at any endeavor I pursued.

Family, backgrounds, and even past mistakes can all shape and influence your story. You could have individuals close to you that want you to live according to their agenda. You may be tempted to limit yourself based on your surroundings. Your past failures may try to coerce you into settling for less than what you're capable of. Whether you realize it or not, your life experiences can linger in your mind and distort your perception of who you really are. It took some time for me to understand this concept but it wasn't until I did, that I was able to begin the process of repairing the damage that had been done to my self-identity. My story was influenced by the thought that anything I said would be wrong. This stemmed from my childhood. It's amazing how huge of an impact our experiences as children can have on our lives. Many of the things we do as adults, whether consciously or unconsciously, are rooted from our childhood. As a kid, I was quiet, reserved, and never had much to say—partially because I was naturally introverted, but mainly because I felt comfortable hiding myself in silence. When I started school, I had a speech impediment that made it challenging for me to pronounce certain words correctly. I had to see a speech therapist who assisted me with word pronunciation. As a kid I didn't think anything of it because it was *my* normal. I would say words and never gave thought to whether I was saying them correctly—until I began to hear from others that my pronunciations were incorrect. As a child, it's very easy to take things in a literal sense. That's exactly what I did—instead of understanding that I was just pronouncing words wrong I interpreted it as every time I said something...*I* was wrong. Which began a process of negative conditioning that built a mental prison in my mind.

My hesitancy to speak up as a child was thinking that I'd embarrass myself. As a teenager, I chose to stay quiet, fearing the rejection that I might receive from others. As an adult, I was afraid to speak my mind, afraid I'd say something wrong. This narrative replayed in my mind over and over again until it reached the point that I not only thought I'd say something wrong, but I also began to believe that there was something wrong with me.

If you tell a lie big enough, loud enough and often enough…sooner than later you'll begin to believe it, and it will disguise itself as truth. That lie eventually becomes your story. What you say to *yourself* has the greatest influence on what you believe. In other words, you can condition yourself to believe something that has no truth to it just by resonating the idea. This became my struggle. My story was built on a lie that echoed in my mind, which carried over into my adult life. My mind became a prison that incarcerated my potential. I was full of great things but was afraid to release them because of the sabotaging story in my head.

Have you ever felt like you were worthless? Ever found it hard to identify what makes you special? Have you ever searched for reasons to love yourself but couldn't seem to find any? —This is where my thoughts had taken me—afraid to speak, not connecting with others, and struggling to love myself.

I was convinced that there was something wrong with me and found myself fighting a silent battle that no one knew about. Depression set it. A phenomenon, that when it gets a grip on you it can choke the life out of you. It robs you of your joy and makes you feel defenseless. When it would hit me, I'd lose my motivation, my ambition, and any hope of a better tomorrow. I felt purposeless and would question my own significance. I was surrounded by family, friends, and in a world full of nearly 7 billion people. Yet, I felt lonely. As if I were in a world all by myself. I didn't want to be around other people, but any time I was, you couldn't tell what I was dealing with. I'd fake a smile and mask the pain pretending to be ok. I bottled in my emotions thinking no one would understand how I felt. It seemed like a dark cloud was hovering over my head that would just drain the energy out of me. I'd go to sleep tired, wake up tired, and there were days when I didn't want to leave the bed. From the outside looking in, I was blessed and had so many things going for me, but when your mind is consumed by lies you can overlook your blessings and find yourself in a miserable state.

Day after day, I felt insignificant and purposeless, and subconsciously, I would constantly find reasons to try to validate these feelings. My thoughts would justify what I believed was wrong with me. I wanted to be free from these feelings, but during times like this it was hard to escape my thoughts. I found myself suffering in hopelessness. Suffering is the result of your thoughts being focused in the wrong direction. It's an indication that you're out of harmony with yourself, and that you're not in tune with the real you. Being depressed was not the real me, but depression has a way of making you think that you're *"supposed"* to feel the way that you do. The reality is that no one is ever supposed to feel this way. This is not living. We were born to live. We were born to come alive.

I was hoping for things to change. Where was my happiness? Where was my joy? Where was my passion for living? They were taken from me by the lies that continued to repeat themselves in my head. In order for a change to take place, I had to be the one to initiate it. A change in *your* life always starts with a change within *you*. To get my life back I first had to change my story.

How did I change my story? I'll explain it this way—back in school, every great teacher I had would say to ask as many questions as possible. They would say things like, *"There's no such thing as a dumb question. The only crazy questions are the ones that are never asked."* Why would they advise students to ask questions? Because there's so much possibility in questions—think about it. Knowledge is not driven by answers...it's driven by questions. Without questions we wouldn't develop new knowledge or create new things. Questions open up new worlds of possibilities. As it relates to our stories and how we view ourselves, we often develop the habit of just accepting what life or the lies in our head offer us instead of doing our own investigation and confirming the truth for ourselves. Without investigating, you'll find yourself living with a negative story and adjusting who you are to accommodate things that were never meant to be. So in order to change my story was I started asking questions instead of accepting answers. In other words I began challenging the negative and patronizing things I had always believed about myself. Which led to me discovering more of the real me.

Until this point, I never challenged the story in my head. I didn't question the validity of what I thought about myself. I simply defined myself based on what I heard in my mind. Which was the reason why I developed such a negative story—but I changed that. They say perception is reality—and my perception became my reality. But truth always supersedes reality. What it looks like may not be what it is. I started living my life and seeing myself from the lens of truth.

Depression put me in a place where I felt broken. When things are broken you take them back to the designer to get fixed. When a car is not functioning properly you take it back to the manufacturer to get it repaired. I had to connect with my Creator to fix my brokenness. Depression helped me establish my relationship with God, and after I began to grow spiritually I began to realize that I am fearfully and wonderfully made, that I did matter, and that I had reasons to love myself. I began to understand that there is something special within me and that I do have something to offer to the world. This became my story.

I started doing the things that the voices in my head told me I couldn't do. I started speaking and encouraging others. I started inching out of my comfort zone, expressing my thoughts and ideas. I began to notice that people would respond in positive ways. My words added value to others. People benefitted from my insights. I began to realize that the story that once ruled my world was nothing but a lie. It was at this point that I started unlearning everything that I thought about myself and began reinventing who I was. Looking back, I would have never guessed that the thing that I was afraid of the most was actually the area I was gifted in. I lived in a story that belittled my voice and what it could do for the others, but changing my story amplified my voice and it now echoes inspiration to dreamers all across the world. Which goes to show that the things that we often feel insecure about are the very things that hold our strengths.

Many people spend so much of their lives running away from the very thing that they should be running towards—their real self. They hide from it, avoid it, and reject it when they should be working to actively express it. When you express the real you, you engage with the world and open your life up to opportunities for learning, exploration, and adventure. Not only that, but you also have to learn to accept yourself for who you are. There's power in acceptance. Acceptance doesn't mean that you ignore your shortcomings or that you stop changing your life for the better. It means that you stop the self-sabotaging and finding fault with yourself. No more burying yourself in the grave of misery. Never be ashamed of who you are. Accept yourself for better and for worse. Your power is found in loving and being your authentic self.

What limited beliefs have you allowed to control your life? What identity have you placed on yourself that was never meant to be? What story do you continue to repeat in your mind that has never been confirmed to be true? Again, the hardest prison to escape is your mind. When you win the battles within your mind, you'll win your battles in life. Marianne Williamson once said, *"Our deepest fear is not that we are inadequate. Our deepest fear is that we are powerful beyond measure. It is our light, not our darkness, that most frightens us. We ask ourselves, 'Who am I to be brilliant, gorgeous, talented, fabulous?' Actually, who are you not to be, you are a child of God. Your playing small does not serve the world. There is nothing enlightened about shrinking so that other people won't feel insecure around you. We were born to make manifest the glory of God that is within us. It is not just in some of us; it is in everyone. And as we let our own light shine, we unconsciously give permission to other people to do the same. As we are liberated from our own fear, our presence automatically liberates others."*

Change your story and give yourself permission to be the real you. Your work is to discover the truth in your world and then with all your heart, give yourself to it and reinvent who you are. Find out how you fit in the world and share the story that only you can tell. Self-identity is an evolving process that happens throughout your lifetime. Decide the person that you want to be and stay true to yourself. You'll find out more of who you are when you begin to get rid of who you're not. Your story is one of success—you are alive to do great things. It's time to for you to change your narrative and shine your light. When you get rid of who you're not...you'll become the real you.

THE WELL KNOWN

SECRET

EACH NEW DAY CAN BE THE BEGINNING OF ANYTHING YOU WANT

The only limits you have are the ones that you choose to acknowledge in your own mind. Coming alive and leveling up your life calls for you to look beyond what you currently are and to visualize yourself as what you can become. You have to dream big to see big results. Thinking small will have you living a miniature size life, but dreaming big will open up your life to new experiences. In this chapter, you'll discover how dreaming big can transform your life.

I'm sure you've seen elephants being used for hard labor in various countries around the world. Carrying huge loads and transporting things that normally would be done by huge machinery. Do you know how they train these elephants? How do you restrain an animal that weighs over 8,000 pounds? What the elephant handlers realize is that they can't overpower the elephants physically. They're way too strong and powerful. However, they can overpower them mentally by controlling their minds.

When the elephant is young, a rope, weighing around 150 pounds is tied around its front leg. At this age and size, the elephant hasn't built up the strength to free itself from the rope. It tries to escape by yanking the rope, chewing on the rope and tugging back and forth. After much effort and many attempts the elephant is still tied down. Each attempt discourages the elephant until it finally surrenders. It's at this moment that the elephant becomes controlled by the rope.

Because of the failed attempts the elephant strongly believes that there is no possible way that it can escape the rope, and it begins to accept the fate of being limited and held back by the rope. This limit becomes stamped in the elephants' beliefs, and the handlers are successful in using the ropes to control it. Even when the elephant matures into an adult it still is controlled by this limited and imaginary belief that it can't break free.

In the same way that a rope can restrict the elephant, we too can be restricted by doubt. Many people live life with their potential tied down. They are gifted, talented, skilled, and capable of doing big and great things. Yet they become confined by their self-made limitations. They think small and put limits on what's possible.

What separates those that succeed and those that fail? Do some people have a "*super*" gene in their DNA? Are there some people that are just lucky at what they do? Are there only a select group of individuals that are capable of becoming high achievers? The answer is No—It's easy to think that others are more capable than you are, but the reality is that you too have the ability to succeed.

It all starts in your mind. You become what you think. As simple as it may sound, it has power and influence over our lives. What we consistently think on will determine what we eventually become. Thoughts of confidence form into success. Thoughts of fear create outcomes of failure. Thoughts of doubt evolve into poor performance. Thoughts of gratitude shape your happiness. Whatever thoughts you choose to entertain inside of your mind will ultimately be revealed in your life. In knowing this, if you want to do big things then you must think big.

There is no such thing as thinking too big. The only dreams that are ridiculous are the ones that you choose not to pursue. The great orator Les Brown says, "*Most people fail in life not because they aim too high and they miss, but because they aim too low and they hit.*" They settle and never get what they deserve. They never achieve what they're capable of. They never get to see what their life truly could become—because they think small and aim low.

Why do many people aim low in life? One challenge is that many people develop low expectations for themselves. They never connect with their true identity and end up settling for a life that is less than the one that they are capable of living. They don't believe in their worth and never buy into the fact that their life has significance. They become led by their insecurities instead of being led by their purpose. They accept whatever life offers even if it makes them unhappy.

Another challenge is that many people tend to stop believing in possibilities. Life has a way of killing your impulse to dream. It has a way of making your dreams seem impossible. It has its way of making you doubt your abilities. We all experience failure which can be a tough pill to swallow. Failures are discouraging, disappointments are frustrating, and setbacks can often deter you from pursuing new goals. We all go through something, we all have a story, and every story is full of adversity. One thing about adversity is that it can kill your ambition if you allow it to. It's because of the challenges that life presents that many people tend to lose touch of their imagination.

A third challenge is that many people never realize the potential they have for change, growth, and improvement. They believe that life *"is what it is"* and eventually become satisfied with just getting by. They become content with the way things are and settle for an average life. Instead of standing out in the world they'd rather fit in to avoid having to face their doubts.

It's because of these challenges that many people find themselves, either consciously or unconsciously, thinking small and aiming low in life.

However, these challenges can be overcome. You can break the cycle of aiming low. How? You have to use your weapon of mass creation.

USE YOUR MIND

The hardest prison to escape is the one in your mind. Some of the world's greatest ideas have never been brought to the public because they are trapped in the minds of individuals that can't overcome their self-made limitations. To come alive and experience greater levels of personal achievement, you have to not only change the way you see yourself, but also change the way you see the world around you. You have to reach a new understanding of how you fit in the world.

Envisioning yourself in a greater light and thinking highly of what you're capable of accomplishing. You have to raise the bar in your mind, take off the limits in your imagination, and create a vision for your life. It takes the same amount of energy to think big as it does to think small. So why not think big? You become what you think. So, create the highest and biggest vision possible. Don't be afraid to stretch your mind and ask for more out of life. Jessie Rittenhouse wrote a poem that describes this:

"I bargained with Life for a penny,
And Life would pay no more,
However I begged at evening
When I counted my scanty store;

For Life is just an employer,
He gives you what you ask,
But once you have set the wages,
Why, you must bear the task.

I worked for a menial's hire,
Only to learn, dismayed,
That any wage I had asked of Life,
Life would have paid."

In other words—*you have not because you ask not.* Many people don't realize this until they're older in age. They live most of their life without dreaming big. Opportunities, possibilities, and the great adventures of life are often missed. They do things they don't enjoy, work jobs that they hate, and sit on abilities that the world needs. You have to decide to break the cycle of limited thinking. Decide that you're not going to play life small. Decide to dream big, and never stop discovering more about yourself and exploring what's possible.

Don't do what most people do which is deciding to do what's easy or what seems logical. There is no magic in logic. There is no faith in logic. There's a Hebrews scripture that says, *"Faith is the substance of things hoped for and the evidence of things not seen."* If you can see it, it's not faith. Great things happen when we take on the impossible and pursue the illogical. You can't be afraid to use

24

your imagination. Have you ever stopped to think about how powerful your imagination is? Imagination was the tool that Steve Jobs and his team at Apple used to create the iPhone, which revolutionized the world. It was the instrument that Jay-Z played that transformed his life of running the streets with drug dealers to closing deals in the boardroom with CEO's. Imagination was the canvas that Maya Angelou used to express her world and inspire others through her riveting poetry.

We sometimes forget how powerful the mind really is. Albert Einstein said, *"Logic will get you from point A to point B, but imagination will take you anywhere."* Your greatest tool to creating an amazing life is your imagination. You can literally paint a picture in your mind of a future that does not exist and bring it into existence. You still need to put forth the necessary efforts to make it happen, but it all starts in the mind.

The great things in life don't only come through our senses. Some of the most amazing experiences we have are generated inside the mind. Your imagination gives you the ability to fly into new worlds of possibility. It gives you vision beyond what's in sight. It allows you to see things that may not exist. It gives you the freedom to create, the ability to bring to mind things that are not present in reality. No matter where you find yourself, it always presents you with the opportunity to step outside of the present moment and step into something greater. It is the laboratory that generates ideas, the workshop that constructs dreams, and the drawing board that sketches visions. It's what you use to shape your life.

Everything begins in your imagination—from ideas, to achievements, to victories, to inventions and businesses. Whether they are big or small, they all begin in your mind. This is what makes your thoughts so powerful and you have full permission to use this power.

Believe in your big dreams even when others think you're crazy. You may get talked about but never scale down your vision to please others. Most people have a tendency to disbelieve anything they don't understand. The Wright Brothers announced that they built the first airplane and everyone thought they were crazy. Paulo Coelho, the author of the international best seller *The Alchemist*, was sent to a mental asylum as a teenager when his parents thought he was sick in the mind for wanting to be an author. People thought Harriet Tubman was out of her mind for risking her life to save enslaved people through the Underground Railroad. Not everyone will understand your vision. When others try to dissuade you from thinking big, you have to stick to your guns and continue to dream big. As your vision gets larger you'll notice your circle will get smaller. That's because small-minded people can't understand big dreamers. It's like you're speaking a different language. They just don't comprehend big ideas. Some people are just set in their ways and have no desire for more in life. This is why it's important to stay surround by ambitious and bold individuals who challenge the status quo and believe in doing the impossible.

Don't base what's possible on your past or even your present. You can take your life anywhere you dream of, doesn't matter where you come from, what matters most is where you're going. Many people have the tendency to think small because they believe that we are each products of our environment. I believe there's some truth to this statement, but not in its entirety. Our environment and upbringing do play a large role in our lives, and have some influence on the type of person we become. However, I don't believe that they are the determining factors to the type of life we live. We become products of our expectations. When you raise your level of thinking, you can raise your level of awareness in life. You see more, you become more, and you achieve more. Take the film director Ryan Coogler for example, born and raised in Oakland, California. A place much known for its streets flooded with drugs, gangs, and violence. If Ryan would have limited himself to his environment, there's a good chance that he could have found himself running the streets. Instead, he had greater expectations than what he saw with his physical eyes and used his imagination to help him create a new reality. This helped him create blockbuster films such as *Creed* and *Black Panther.* All because he expected more and he filled his mind with thoughts that affirmed his expectation.

"Don't conform to the world, but be transformed by the renewing of your mind." (Romans 12:2) Meaning, you may have grown up in poverty, but if you develop a millionaire's mindset you can create a new reality. You may not come from an educated family, but, if you aim high, you can earn your doctorate. You may not have traveled outside of your city, but, if you keep the adventure alive in your mind, you can travel the world with your dreams. Being open to possibilities gives

you a different rulebook for your life. You see things differently when you dream big. You interpret situations and experiences differently. Never downgrade your dreams to fit your reality. Instead, upgrade your vision to match your destiny.

THINKING BIG IS A CHOICE

We are limited only by the thoughts that we choose. In other words, the only limits in your mind are the ones that you choose to acknowledge. You have the ability to choose between thinking small or dreaming big. We are all born as naturally curious individuals. In fact, as children we are fascinated and led by our imagination. A child isn't controlled by doubt. You ask them what they want to be when they grow up and they believe they can do anything. A singer, the president, a movie star, a doctor…they're not concerned about failing, life getting in the way, or what other people think. Children don't comprehend the meaning of limitations. Think about how much joy a child has when they use their imagination. Think about how much life they radiate when they don't put limits on what's possible. As adults, we often lose this impulse to dream. We lose the courage to try new things. We stop exploring greater possibilities. Why is this? It's because the challenges of life can sometimes influence you to think that your options are limited and you have to stay within the boundaries of what's familiar. *Don't think too big, they'll call you crazy. Be more realistic and stick to what's normal*—but the reality is you can choose to look at your life differently. You can choose to look beyond your right now and envision what your life can become. You can be a kid again and let your imagination excite you. There's open access to positive change and transformation in your life and it's found in your mind.

Thinking big is a choice that only you can make. You may not have every step calculated and every move choreographed, but that doesn't have to stop you from dreaming. You simply have to use your imagination. Your feet will never go anywhere that your mind hasn't already been, so venture to your dreams first in your imagination. Whatever you want for your life, you must first see it in your mind. You can achieve whatever the mind can conceive. You just have to focus on allowing your mind to be free and choose to dream big.

YOU HAVE THE ABILITY TO GROW

The challenge with many people is that they become too familiar with the word impossible. They automatically assume what can't be done and what will never work. Which causes them to never try anything new or different. If you measure everything solely by your own impressions and beliefs, based only by what you've done in your past, you'll be limiting yourself. If you only see life from your own perspective and never expand your horizons, then you make the mistake of believing that you could never evolve into something greater. The biggest room in the world is the room for improvement, and we each have access to that room. You have to decide to step into it even if it seems risky. When you let go of your objections, you'll set the stage for growth to occur in your life.

In the same way that a caterpillar metamorphoses into a butterfly, you too can transform your life. No matter what life currently looks like, always see yourself experiencing greater. One common belief that every achiever shares is the belief that they have the ability to create a tomorrow that is better than the present. They don't base their potential on their past and not even on their present. They find hope in what they believe is possible.

Your capabilities are not fixed. New talents can be learned. Skills can be developed. You have to open your mind to the idea of expanding yourself. Who you are and where you've come from is your story. Own it, but don't be limited by it. You can always reinvent who you are. In order to open up our minds to the exciting world of new possibilities, we have to be willing to break the rules of our past. Instead of being a victim of your history...be a creator of your future. Have a vision of a greater tomorrow and understand that growth is possible.

CREATE YOUR VISION

Create a vision of the future that produces passion. Create a vision of who you want to become. A vision that wakes you up in the morning, gets you excited, and adds meaning to your life. Create a vision of exactly what you want. No limits. No boundaries. No restrictions. Set a goal that's beyond your reach and that stretches out the best in you. If you set a goal that is attainable without much effort and much work, you'll be aiming for something that could be below your true talent and potential...instead aim for the stars. The future belongs to those who dream big.

You'll get a peek at what's possible when you stop being limited by your past, look further than your doubts, and disconnect from your fears. Your vision may scare you at first, as it calls you out of your comfort zone and charges you to do things that you're not used to, but don't shut it down. It will eventually lead you to something worthwhile. One of the best things you can do is to give yourself permission to dream. To create a vision for your life that's clear and compels you to take action.

When you create a vision for your life, it often serves as a reminder of what you're capable of. Visions come from within us—from a part of us that doesn't believe in limitations. Deep down inside of you, you know what you can become and what direction you want to take your life. The average person spends their entire life running away from it, but, if you remove the blockages that prevent you from seeing what you can become, you'll take your life above average. You'll astonish yourself by what you're capable of accomplishing. I spent much time thinking small and running away from the vision that was calling me to become a speaker. I was afraid to think big. I assumed, since I had never done it, then I couldn't do it. This was a limited belief. I was the elephant that was tied down by the rope. Allowing my doubts to control my life. When you doubt your power you give power to your doubt. It was when I used my mind and started dreaming big, that I began to realize I was stronger than my doubts. I realized that these imaginary limitations were something I made and created, and, since I created them, I could destroy them. My dreams began to influence me to do things I never could have imagined.

There is something within you waiting to be born. Take the limits off of your imagination and establish a new vision for where your life can go. What is it that you really want to do with your life? What is that idea that gets you excited? It's time to break the cycle of thinking small and to live the rest of your life dreaming big. If you want your days to be filled with passion and excitement, dream big and create a vision for your life.

The one thing that every person wants is freedom—to live life unrestrained and not trapped in the prison of doubt. Your imagination gives you this opportunity. You can shape your world by what you create in your mind. What you view as being possible is a vital key to your success in every aspect of your life. Creating inner boundaries will sabotage true lasting success, no matter how gifted or talented you may be. You'll be that 8-ton elephant being held down by a

100lb rope. You'll be that person missing opportunities because they don't see their potential.

Change your perception of what's possible and give yourself permission to dream big. The moment that you stop striving for more in life will become the moment that you'll start accepting less. If you choose to dream big and determine in your mind to always seek more, you'll find that there's always more that you can get out of life.

It only takes one sound idea to transform your life. Just think of the single ideas that have changed the world—there was a time when airplanes didn't exist, there was a time when automobiles didn't exist, there was a time when Facebook didn't exist, and as hard as it is to believe there was a time when cell phones did not exist—but they all began as an idea. Some ideas may seem impossible, but ideas backed with faith and action are what transform our world. You have within you an idea that can transform your world and the world around you, but in order to unleash this idea you have to say yes to dreaming big.

SHAKE UP THE
WORLD

YOU CAN HAVE ANYTHING YOU SET YOUR MIND TO…IF, AND ONLY IF, YOU LOSE THE BELIEF THAT YOU CAN'T HAVE IT

The biggest factor of success is how you view yourself. What you think you're capable of accomplishing will have a direct influence on what your life's outcome. In order to achieve at a high level your self-esteem has to be strong enough to carry the weight of success. You will only rise to the level of success that your self-esteem can absorb. In this chapter, you'll discover how you can strengthen your belief in yourself and be confident in your pursuit towards achievement.

Growing up my mother would always share with me how my grandfather was a big fan of the legendary boxer Muhammad Ali. So by the time I started boxing as a teenager, Ali wasn't just my favorite boxer…he was my favorite athlete. I'd get on YouTube and be amazed with his fights and interviews. In case you didn't know, Ali was the unofficial original trash talker in sports. Of course, athletes have always talked trash since the beginning of competitive sports, but Ali was the one that would say it on camera and made *"trash talking"* mainstream. He said what he meant and meant what he said. He'd call out the round he was going to knock out his opponent, and would backup everything he said. He had style, charisma, and was undoubtedly confident.

He would write poems that highlighted how confident he was…

"I'm gonna float like a butterfly and sting like a bee, your fist can't hit what your eyes can't see…rumble young man rumble."

"Last night I wrestled with an alligator, I tussled with a whale, I handcuffed lighting and threw thunder in jail, I'm bad man!"

"I murdered a rock, injured a stone, hospitalized a brick, I'm so mean I make medicine sick."

Ali defied the odds when people said he was either too young or too old to be a champion. He shut up his critics when it seemed like no one took him seriously. He went on to change not just the sport of boxing but the entire world of sports.

One of Ali's quotes helped me understand more about his approach to each fight. It helped me get a different glimpse of what was really going on when he spoke in front of the cameras and promote his abilities. It's a quote that has stuck with me since the first time I heard it. He said, *"I called myself the greatest before I even knew I was."*

Think about that...

Before he stepped in the ring, before the lights were set up, before the cameras were running—he called himself the greatest.

Before the journalists new his name, before his critics began to doubt him, before his opponents were even selected—he called himself the greatest.

Before he became a professional, before he traveled the world doing interviews, and before his fans cheered him on—he called himself the greatest.

With every word he spoke, Ali affirmed himself. With every poem he delivered he manifested his victory into existence. Because he identified himself as *"The greatest"*, he *"shook up the world"* and became just what he believed himself to be.

What can we learn from this? What lesson can we take away from Muhammad Ali talking himself into being confident? What we can learn is that our words have the power to create either life or death. They have the power to shift your attitude and can influence you to take confident steps towards your goals. They have the power to either make you feel defeated or make you feel determined. It's all a matter of how you communicate with yourself.

Any time you think about doing something extraordinary, there will often be a voice in your head trying to convince you that you can't do it...

You're too young. You're too old. Not smart enough. Not good enough. Not qualified. Not creative enough. You don't have the money. Don't have the time. You've never done it before. You failed the last time you tried.

This is the voice of doubt and whatever major goal you decide to pursue, there's always going to be this voice echoing in your mind trying to convince you that you will fail. Doubt will make you feel inadequate. It will discourage you from moving your life forward and it will often keep you from taking action. It's a battle that many people fight daily. The world renown artist, Michelangelo, doubted himself when asked to paint the now famous ceiling of the Vatican's Sistine Chapel because he considered himself to be a sculptor not a painter. After flunking out of college and unsure about what he wanted to do with his life, the actor Denzel Washington doubted his ability to travel the world and speak to millions of people when a woman in the beauty salon predicted that he had a future in reaching people in a positive way. Doubt will give you an unclear view of what's possible. It will block you from seeing what you're truly capable of. When you doubt yourself, you end up like a wave in the sea being tossed and pushed around by the wind, with no true control over what direction your life takes. Doubt will diminish your confidence and sabotage your ability to reach new levels in life.

It's a hindering force that not only comes from within, but it can also come from those around you. This can in return influence you to doubt yourself. Friends and family may try to convince you to reconsider your abilities. There may be people that will say anything to make you question yourself. It's unfortunate, but there are some people who are unhappy with their lives and to temporarily alleviate their personal frustration they like to take their pain out on others. You can find some of these people in the comments section on social media. They're like hecklers in the stands saying nearly any and everything to get a response. But in the end, it doesn't matter what anybody else thinks. What matters is what you believe. Regardless of where the doubt comes from, you must understand this important truth: The voice that tells you that you can't do it...is a liar. It's your job to prove it wrong.

I CAN DO THIS

The Chinese philosopher, Confucius, once said, *"Those that think they can and those that think they can't are both usually right."* When you tell yourself that you can't do something then you won't. But when you tell yourself that you can do something then you will. Our greatest battles are those within our own mind.

There's an old parable that describes a grandfather teaching his grandson about life... "A fight is going on inside of you." He says to the boy. "It's a vicious fight between two wolves. One is evil—he is negativity, self-doubt, inferiority, inadequacy, and insecurity. The other is positivity—he is hope, truth, confidence, assurance, certainty, and faith. The same fight is going on inside of every other person you'll ever see." The grandson then asked his grandfather, "Which wolf will win?" The grandfather replied, "The one that you feed."

When you go from feeling motivated to feeling doubtful it's because you are feeding the wrong wolf. When your attitude shifts from being confident to feeling intimidated it's because you are feeding the wrong wolf. When you lose your ambition to pursue the things that make you come alive, it's because you're feeding the wrong wolf. It's the negative wolf that has you placing limitations on your capabilities and causing you to doubt what's possible. You are not your true self when you feed the wrong wolf. You have to work daily to feed the right wolf in order to move your life forward.

What do you feed the wolf with? You feed it with your thoughts and with the words that you choose to say to yourself. You feed it with the daily conversation that you have within your own head. As you feed one then by nature you begin to starve the other. As you feed your mind the truth about yourself, the lies will lose their influence. As you feed your mind faith, the doubts will simultaneously lose the power they seek to have in your life.

Your mindset plays a huge role in your ability to achieve. In order to develop a positive mental attitude you have to think and speak positively and be certain about who you are and what you can do. Your level of control over your mind will determine the type of life you live. It's the quality of your thoughts that will determine the quality of your life. When you have a dream, you have to develop the habit of telling yourself that you can achieve it. This is why there are some individuals that appear to be in hopeless situations and still succeed when the odds are stacked against them. Take Frederick Douglas for example, he was born into slavery and later separated from his mother at a young age. He taught himself how to read in secret by observing the writings of others. He would get beat by his slave master when it became known that he was attempting to learn. Through it all, he eventually rebelled, escaped slavery, and ended up writing his own autobiography and became one of the great orators in history...all because he fed the right wolf and convinced himself that he could do it.

Our daily attitude and outlook on life are both personal choices. You have the ability to choose what state of mind you'll have each day. You get to choose what you focus on. You get to choose how you view situations and interpret your challenges. You may not be able to stop or control all of the negative thoughts from passing through your mind, but you can stop those negative thoughts from controlling you. It's all a matter of you deciding that you are going to continue to affirm and believe in who you are and what you can do.

You can talk yourself into a victory. You can talk yourself into being confident. You can talk yourself into believing in the power of you. There may be times when you doubt yourself and may be uncertain of your ability to achieve. It's during these moments that the conversation in your head has to shift towards success.

The very first time I was asked to speak at an event, I quickly realized how much influence your self-talk has on your ability to achieve. I was asked to be a keynote speaker after a family friend heard me share a few encouraging words at my uncle's funeral. I immediately shut the idea down. I thought, *Me! I don't have anything special to say...I could never do that!* I was afraid to say yes because I wanted to avoid having to speak in public. I had just gone through the anxious experience of speaking at my uncle's funeral. I didn't want to go through another similar experience of being in front of a group of people where everyone's eyes and attention were directed towards me. I tried to decline the offer, but she practically told me that I didn't have a choice in the matter and she was going to let her team know that I would be speaking. So...I was coerced into speaking. It was one of those things where I didn't really commit to it, but she wasn't going to accept "*NO*" for an answer.

The night before the event I was flat out nervous. There was this huge rush of anxiety running through me. I remember thinking, "*WHAT DID I GET MYSELF INTO?!*". I was upset with myself for even committing to doing this. There was expected to be over 300 people attending the event and that number intimidated me every time I thought about it. All I could think about was everything that could go wrong...*What if I freeze? What if I stumble on stage? What if what I say makes no sense at all?* Then the conversation in my head shifted from fear to doubt...*Who are you? Why would anyone want to listen to you? Do you really think you have anything to say?*

They say public speaking is the biggest fear that people have, even greater than death. Meaning most people would rather be the one in the casket than the one delivering the eulogy. I was feeling every bit of this fear first hand. There I was in my apartment, stressed and completely overwhelmed, pacing the floor. Hours had gone by. My heart was throbbing and felt like it was about to explode through my chest. I had no idea how I was going to pull this off. I wanted to escape.

My mind seemed to be running a mile a minute with no sign of it slowing down. Then, everything shifted with one action...I started talking to myself.

Calm down, you can do this. I couldn't even count the number of times that I repeated that statement, but as I continued to say it out loud, I began to feel the weight of doubt lifting off me. The grip of anxiety started to release. My attitude about speaking began to change and I could hear my thoughts clearly.

*You can do this...You can do this...You can do this...*Over and over again, I repeated that statement like it was a lyric in a song. I was feeling optimistic about speaking. I was now thinking positively about what would happen. I became hopeful about how things would turn out.

I began believing that someone would be positively impacted by what I had to say. Someone needed to be inspired by my message. Someone was waiting to hear my message. The negative thoughts continued to try to discourage me, but they didn't have the same effect. My mind had now become so focused on the thought that I could actually do this, that I didn't even acknowledge the negativity. I would hear the very same negative thoughts that I heard fifteen minutes before this moment, but the effect and how they made me feel was the complete opposite. My entire attitude began to change simply because I changed what I said to myself.

Before, I was dreading the entire event. Now I was looking forward to it. The only thing that had changed was my self-talk.

I woke up the next morning with a confidence that I had never felt before. Everything that I doubted became my confidence. I stood on stage delivering my message, and felt free. I felt at ease. I felt like I was in my element.

When I was able to reflect on what this experience taught me, I thought about the impact I was able to make. After the event, there were dozens of people who approached me raving about how my speech inspired them and how resonating my words were. I realized how the doubts that I battled the night before could have prevented these people from experiencing breakthroughs in their lives. I also thought about the fact that *I was invited to speak.* I didn't ask to be the keynote speaker, or make a request to be apart of the event. I was invited by someone who saw something in me, even when I couldn't see it in myself. It's important to realize that just because you can't see something that's within you, it doesn't mean that it isn't there. Doubt will blind you of your abilities and prevent you from seeing what's possible. We oftentimes *"sleep on our potential"*—diminishing our value and discrediting our skills. You can't allow your doubts to cause you to overlook your greatness.

You are talented and full of unique abilities. There's a gift within you that will enable you to do amazing things and change your life. This experience taught me that life will never change until you first change the way you talk to yourself.

Changing self-talk is difficult for many people to comprehend and apply to their lives. They've spent their entire lives doubting themselves. They've had family members tell them they'll never be somebody. People have told them they'll never do anything. They've dealt with things that have literally robbed them of their confidence, and they go through life feeling insignificant, inadequate, and insecure. Maybe you can relate to this. Maybe you know what it's like to go through life doubting yourself. Maybe you know what it's like to be anxious about putting yourself out there and sharing your passions with the world. Maybe you feel like you are missing something that others seem to have…Let me keep it real with you: YOU ARE ENOUGH. You are gifted and capable of living out your greatest potential. The worst thing to do is to grow accustomed to doubting yourself and accommodating a life that is less than the one that you are capable of living. You are better than this and you are greater than this. We all hear the voice of doubt, but again, that doesn't mean we have to be controlled by it. There may be a million voices in your head telling you that you can't do something, but you must be the voice that says you can. Instead of being critical of yourself, try encouraging yourself. You'll never live a victorious life while speaking defeat. Your words have power. They have the ability to build you up or break you down, but the amazing part is that you get to decide which words you will live by. Make a conscious and a deliberate choice to be led by thoughts and words that pull you closer to your dreams instead of pushing you further away.

We each have to learn to get into the habit of believing in and affirming ourselves. Even when things seem tough, you have to be confident in your ability to win in life. Speak the language of success—I CAN. I WILL. IT'S POSSIBLE. Speak confidently and believe that no matter the circumstance, you can figure out how to make things work in your favor. One thing that no one else can control, but you, is the perception that you have of yourself. Other people may have their opinions, but never allow someone's opinion to be your truth. Know that you are somebody. Believe that you are fearfully and wonderfully made. Be confident in what you have to offer to the world and let your words reflect what you believe. Even if your life doesn't currently reflect your dream continue to speak it into existence. Because the thoughts that you choose to acknowledge and the words that you choose to speak will set the tone for your attitude. A successful attitude will lead to successful actions, which eventually lead to successful results. You can talk yourself *into doing things* in the same way you can talk yourself *out of doing things*. You just have to change what you say.

When Muhammad Ali was surrounded by doubt, he defeated Sony Liston to become the heavyweight champion of the world. When everyone believed he would get knocked out, and thought he'd even get killed in the ring, he said "I CAN DO THIS". They said he was too young, he didn't have enough experience, and he was out of his league—but he believed in himself.

After defeating his opponent and silencing his critics, here were his words: *"I'm the champ of the world! I'm the greatest that's ever lived! I upset Sony Liston and I just turned 22 years old! I must be the greatest! I told the world. I talked to God every day. If God is with me nobody can be against me! I shook up the world, I shook up the world, I shook up the world!"*

The best thing you can do is to believe in yourself, and your self-talk should back up what you believe. It's easy to give up on you but you deserve so much more. Even when no one is cheering you on you have to know without a shadow of a doubt that YOU CAN. You may not be the smartest, the strongest, the most talented, the most experienced, or the most qualified but if you continue to speak the language of success you too can shake up the world.

THE POWER
OF A DECISION

YOU ARE ALWAYS ONE DECISION AWAY FROM TRANSFORMING YOUR LIFE

E very decision we make comes with a consequence. Whether we make them intentionally or unintentionally, the choices we make will create outcomes that we have to live with. Decisions can be difficult to make depending on the situation. Especially, when it's a choice between where you should be and where you want to be. When you are clear on your values and what's important to you, it becomes easy to make decisions. In this chapter we are going to get clear on how making clear, congruent, and committed decisions can help you begin the process of living life on your own terms.

WHY SETTLE FOR MISERY?

The waves of water and mud crashed aggressively up against the side of the home and it seemed like at any moment the house could be lifted up and pulled away from its foundation. With every passing second, it seemed like borrowed time for the man that was trapped inside.

The TV screen read in bright red letters, *Breaking News*. I was tuning in to a news coverage of responders working to rescue a man to safety. Here was the scenario: A flash flood struck just outside of Phoenix, Arizona—lifting and destroying nearly everything in its path. Both the rescue responders and the news team were hovering above the home in separate helicopters. It was a ranch style home and the water level forced the man to climb to the roof in order to stay safe. The house was pinned up against a tree, which seemed to be the only thing keeping it from being sucked up by the flood.

You could see the man pacing from one side of the roof to the other, trying to get a sense of what was going on around him. It wasn't long before a member of the rescue team was lowered from the helicopter with a harness and landed on the roof of the home.

Rain was falling from the sky and water continued to violently push up against the home. The two men were now standing on the roof of the house. The rescuer began to point toward the harness giving the man instructions on how to be lifted to safety. For a moment the trapped man stood there looking at the harness then began lifting his head up towards the helicopter. At first, I couldn't determine what had caused the man to just pause and wait to secure the harness around his body, but then he began to gesture, "*NO*" with his hands. You could tell by watching that there was something bothering him. He seemed to be afraid of having to be lifted hundreds of feet into midair and being supported only by the strength of a mere harness.

Eventually, he decided to take the risk, strapped into the harness, and was lifted to safety. After it was all said and done, I began to think about the incident— What was the man thinking? Why didn't he immediately strap on the harness? He could have been seriously hurt or possibly even killed by the flood. Why did he hesitate to act? I don't know exactly what his thoughts were, but I do know that he was dealing with something that each and every single one of us deal with—fear. He found himself in a position where he was in a dangerous and destructive situation, but to get out of it, he had to take a risk, face his fear, and do something that he had never done before.

Can you relate to this man's dilemma? Maybe you've found yourself in an undesirable or destructive position, or maybe this is something you're currently facing. Trust me, you're not alone. If life is so short, why do we do so many things we don't like and like so many things we don't do? There are many people that are unhappy with where they are in life and what they're doing. They spend their lives doing things they don't enjoy, working jobs that make them feel miserable, and never pursue what seems to be calling their name. They're not immersed in the things they truly love and it bothers them to the core. They feel empty, unfulfilled, and frustrated with the same old boring routine. There's even those that know for a fact that the path they're currently taking will soon lead them to a place that will destroy their future, but they're afraid to make a change. Whatever the case may be, we've all been in a place in life where we have a desire for more. Where we want to experience new horizons and accomplish greater things. Where we find ourselves like the trapped man with a harness in front of us, but afraid to grab ahold of it.

The harness was what the trapped man needed to grab ahold of in order to be lifted. The helicopter would elevate him, but the harness would carry him. We each have a vehicle that can elevate our lives—it could be an opportunity, a new career, an idea, a business you want to start, a new lifestyle you want to create, or a greater venture you want to take on. For each person it's different, but the reality is there's a new level we each can reach but we have to grab ahold of the harness to be lifted. The harness is faith, it's belief, it's being confident in your ability to succeed. You have to latch on to this level of certainty, even while realizing the risks that are involved. Going to new levels and reaching greater heights in life comes with its share of uncertainty. There may be more questions than you have answers, but you have to make the decision to go for it even in the face of fear.

Fear can work in two different ways. It can either weigh you down or it can lift you in the air. It all depends on how you use it. Many people aren't living their dreams because they're living their fears. They choose to remain where they are and where they've always been in life because the unknown of doing something different seems too intimidating. Even while the foundation that they stand on seems to decay, unhappy lifestyle, unfulfilling job, damaging relationships, miserable conditions, they don't change. Many people don't like change—even if it's a good change or a change that could potentially improve their life. Why? Because we as people hate to have our comfort disrupted. Changes involve breaking habits, shifting routines and often require work. These changes go against comfort, security, and familiarity, which the average person does not want to lose. Most of all, change comes with risk, and taking risks is something that many people don't like doing.

What's stopping that aspiring author from writing their first book? What's hindering that great vocalist from auditioning their talent? What's preventing that great leader from running for office? In reality, we stop ourselves. We too often talk ourselves out of taking chances and going for the things we love. We convince ourselves that we should not try because of the risks involved. We allow the intimidating feeling of fear to paralyze our potential.

Like we've mentioned before, doubt can rob you of your confidence and contaminate your self-esteem, but it's also important to realize that fear will stop you from taking action—especially towards the things that matter most to you.

We have a natural tendency to want to stick to doing the things that are easy, safe, and comfortable. We want to feel free and secure, and we seek out the things that give us those feelings. The challenge is that in order to get what you've never had, or go where you've never gone, you have to do things that you've never done before. Which is typically outside of your comfort zone and where fear often speaks the loudest.

When we have a wild dream or a crazy idea that we want to pursue, we often think about the worst that could happen. We imagine everything that could go wrong and get intimidated by the responsibility or the expectations that may be placed on us. We dwell on everything that we don't know, the things that we don't have, and the thought of what we lack leaves us anxious and stuck. We overthink things, wondering how our dreams will come together and pan out in our lives. Too many people doubt what's possible and what they're capable of—procrastinating on their ideas and doing meaningful work in their life.

Why do we postpone, put off, or prolong our dreams? Many people never acknowledge their fear and instead tend to blame everything else...*I'm waiting to save up more money. I'm waiting until I get myself together. I'm waiting until I get a little older. I'm waiting until I graduate from school. I'm waiting until my kids leave the house. I'm waiting until I pay off my debt. I'm waiting...I'm waiting...I'm waiting...*

If you really want something, you'll find a way. If not you'll find an excuse.

Honesty is the best policy, and, in moments like this we have to keep it real with ourselves. It's not circumstances or the lack thereof, but many don't take action because of fear. We can't allow our reasons not to act to become bigger than the reasons why we should. If your life is going to have meaning and if you're going to achieve anything worthwhile, you have to be real with yourself and call your own bluff. This is exactly what I had to do...

I found myself in a position where I was apprehensive to take action on my dream. I developed a new story and opened my mind up to new possibilities. I was reinventing myself, but this didn't mean that fear no longer existed. With new levels come new devils. In fact, when you decide to be a better you, be more creative, and do more with your abilities...fear intensifies. The more you try to elevate your life, the more resistance you'll feel. I was afraid of taking a risk and was hesitant to start something new.

Shortly after graduating from college, I was still working for the same company, still in the same position, but I felt different about what I was doing. When you stretch your mind and open it up to new possibilities you'll never feel comfortable going back to your old world. This was the case for me. I started to picture myself doing more, becoming more, and achieving greater than what I was used to. I knew that my dream couldn't be achieved by remaining where I was. I had no true passion for what I was doing. What once was my usual no longer keep me engaged. When you begin to grow in life, you can outgrow situations. I knew I wasn't using my gifts, my talents, and my full abilities. I knew I wasn't where I was supposed to be, but I felt safe and comfortable. I was getting a paycheck at the end of the week that would temporarily relieve my discomfort, but I wasn't excited about what I was doing with my life. I was comfortably dissatisfied—I felt temporarily relieved but undeniably unhappy. No matter how I tried to avoid it, I still had to face the reality that something was missing.

I wasn't being fulfilled, but I did notice an amazing feeling when I was on stage speaking. Something was growing within me to help others realize their true potential and live out their dreams. It felt great to serve. It felt great to inspire dreamers and I started to envision myself being on stage more. Speaking on stage made me feel alive. It brought a feeling that I didn't know I was missing. Then I thought...*Maybe I could actually do this. Maybe I could become a speaker...*

I would contemplate the idea, but I would constantly ask that haunting question that we all ask ourselves...*How? How was I going to get started? How would things work out? How would I be able to provide for myself? How?...How?...How?* Then the "*What if's*" would come to mind— *What if things don't work out? What if it doesn't go as planned? What if I fail?...What if?...What if?* I would dwell on everything that could go wrong.

Many of these concerns are definitely worth considering, but instead of working to confidently find solutions I was fearfully hesitant to take action. I found myself in a position where I was unhappy with where I was, but afraid to step towards where I wanted to be. My heart was being driven by my dream, but my mind was parked because of my fears. I was like the trapped man, in a home that was rapidly falling apart but afraid to grab hold of the harness.

Again, fear can work in two different ways, it can either weigh you down or it can lift you in the air. It all depends on how you use it. The ordinary person is weighed down by fear, but the extraordinary person uses fear to elevate their life. How? They know what they value.

Do you want to be comfortable or do you want to be great? Do you want to make a living or do you want to build a life? Do you want to live your fears or live your dreams? When you are clear on your values it becomes easy to make decisions. If you ever want to change your behavior, change what you value. Change what you consider to be important in your life. Give your dreams priority.

The extraordinary understand that if they don't act, there are greater consequences that can occur. The bigger risk is found in not taking action. You're guaranteed to fail when you don't try. You'll never reach your full potential when you play it safe. There will always be that thought in your mind wondering what your life could have been had you gone for it. We only get one life to live and it's better lived when we decide to live life pursuing the things that make us come alive. The extraordinary realize that the distance between dreams and reality is action, and I too began to realize that if I wanted to become more and achieve more, then I had to make the decision to give myself permission to commit to my dream.

MAKE A DECISION

Decisions are what get things done. Decisions can change the world. Decisions determine destiny. Martin Luther King Jr. decided to stand up for his dream and the consequence was playing a huge role in opening up opportunities for people of color. Will Smith decided to audition for the Fresh Prince, even though he had no prior acting experience, and the consequence was that it launched his successful acting career. Misty Copeland decided to pursue a career as a ballerina dancer and the consequence was that she began to inspire millions of other young women who faced obstacles when chasing their dreams. We could go on and on about many individuals that have made decisions that have completely shifted their lives, but the key is to understand the power of decisions.

You are always one decision away from transforming your life. Sometimes it's the smallest decisions that can change your life forever, but nothing will happen until you decide. At some point you have to make a decision to pursue your dreams, which requires change in your life. If you decide to only pursue the things that you know are going to work because there is no risk, then you're going to leave a lot of opportunities on the table in your life. To find out what you can accomplish in your life you have to decide to stop playing life small and go for it. Again, remember what you value. It's the choice that often scares you the most that typically is the one that will help you grow in life. Making a big life change can be both hard and scary, but there's something even more difficult and more haunting…regret. You don't want to look back over your life and wonder how it could have been had you decided to pursue your major goals in life.

If nothing changes, then nothing changes. Meaning a change in your life starts with a change within you. You have to make a choice to take a chance or your life will never change. Transformation occurs when you become more committed to your dreams than you are to your comfort zone.

The first step to getting somewhere is to decide that you are not going to stay where you are. When I began taking my dreams seriously, I knew that it was time for a change. My desire and ambition became bigger than my doubts and I was able to overcome my fears and apprehension. It was at that point that I made the decision that I was going for it. I made the commitment to live my dream.

START BEFORE YOU'RE READY

Are you more worried about doing things right, or doing the right things? When is it time to stop calculating risk and reward and just do what you know is right? The key to achievement is to start before you're ready. It's not the risk that people are afraid of, it's how they view it. Fear typically is a product of your own judgment and it's in your power to shift that judgment. Don't lie to yourself about the risks that are involved. Do what you can to get in the best possible position to succeed. Believe in yourself enough to know that whatever you face you can overcome. Devote as much of your time and energy as possible to preparing to take your leap of faith, but make the decision to start. Some of the worst decisions we make are the ones based on fear, and not optimism. Don't let the fear of what could go wrong stop you from living your life. Instead, remember what you value and get motivated by everything that could go right.

One common stumbling block that many people face is that they create an unrealistic demand for perfection. They waste time waiting for the right time....the perfect moment...the ideal situation. If you're waiting for the perfect moment you'll end up waiting your entire life because there is no such thing. Life isn't about waiting for the perfect moment, it's about creating your moment.

If your goal is to start a restaurant, don't wait until you're able to have your own location or for someone to hand you the keys to a building. Start selling plates out of your home. Start catering for different events. Start where you are with what you have. You may not have the funds to purchase a food truck or have your own building right now but that doesn't mean you have to put your dreams on a halt. Maybe your dream is to create films. Don't wait until you have all the fancy equipment and the Hollywood level studio. Utilize what you have and express your imagination. Use the camera on your phone, film wherever you can, and share your story with the world. Whatever you dream is, don't use the excuse that you don't have everything that you need, because you have more than you think. There have been people that have come before you that have been able to do more with less. Just get started and things have a way of falling in place.

You never know what could happen or what opportunities could be created from you deciding to start. You never know who you could connect with when you decide to go for it. Trevor Noah, comedian and host of *The Daily Show,* reached international prominence in his career shortly after he started before he was ready. He hosted his debut one-man show when every other comedian thought he was crazy because he didn't have the following. Goes to show that it's not about what others think, it's about what you believe. People support those that are doing, not those that just talk. Getting started showcases your gifts, talents and abilities to the world. Someone could see you operating in your element and could present you with an opportunity that can transform your life. You just never know until you start before you're ready by taking a courageous step towards your vision.

BE COURAGEOUS

Courage is a choice. It's a decision that you make to move beyond that which scares you. It's following your intuition and making yourself available to the larger plan for your life. It's listening to the voice that you have within that's directing you to advance further. Even when everything around you is telling you otherwise, being courageous is being true to your sense of what's right and taking the risk. It's the overcoming of fear, the resistance of fear, the conquering of fear. It's progressively moving towards a worthwhile goal even while being facing some level of risk. To succeed at your dreams you have to make the decision to live a courageous life.

If you look hard enough, you can always find a reason to try to justify not getting started. Which is why the fear of failure has stopped more people than failure itself. Have a desire for more in life and be fueled by your passion.

The great author Napoleon Hill once said, *"Desire is the starting point of any accomplishment."* It's the beginning of a new chapter. It's the act of embracing new possibilities. Leading up to me committing to my dream, I knew that I was unsatisfied with where I was and I also knew that I was the one who had to change it. Life has so much to offer. More than we can even imagine. Why settle just for what life gives you? You can always create more and experience more when you make what you *desire in life*, what you *demand from life*.

Passion is great energy. It's what can make the impossible happen. I wanted to help people create and live abundant lives. As I continued to share inspiration and speak to many people about their challenges, I began to realize how common it was for people to be unhappy with where they were, what they were doing, or in many cases just unhappy with life. I believe that no one should have to go through life feeling hopeless and worthless. Every person deserves to be happy and to have access to live the life of their dreams, but there are many people struggling to find happiness and a sense of purpose. Many people are even struggling to make it appear as if they're not struggling. It's a vicious cycle. This passion began to evolve within me to help others find purpose in and through their dreams. As I began to realize for my own life, we each have unique abilities to offer to the world and we come alive when we operate in our passions.

We hear it daily—do what you're passionate about, follow your passion, do what you love. But rarely do I hear passion being described in its true meaning. To have a passion for something does mean that you love and enjoy it, but passion is far deeper than that. The word passion comes from the Latin word *passio*, which actually means *"to suffer or to endure"* Meaning the root of the word passion is suffering—for example, *The Passion of Christ.* When you say that you are passionate about something, you are describing something that you are willing to suffer for in order to have—something that you're willing to endure in order to acquire. This is why I encourage many people that are trying to identify their passions not to consider solely, *What you like, love, and enjoy*—but instead, *What work are you willing to suffer for? What means so much to you that you are willing to endure in order to make it happen?*

Knowing that there are many people struggling, suffering, and being robbed of their greatest life because of fear and life's challenges stirred up my passion for helping others become their best selves. This helped me find the courage to commit to my dream.

Desire and passion can be considered the spark that ignites meaningful work. There is strength and power to be found in passion and desire. When you love something so much that you are willing to set aside all forms of logic to get it...that's when you'll achieve the impossible. When you desire something so deeply that you are willing to set aside common sense to obtain it...that's when you'll become a game changer.

There's a story about a chief warrior who went to take back his tribe's island.

Knights had overtaken the island from his ancestors, but the chief was inspired to win it back after hearing about the treasure that was on the island. There were diamonds, gold, and rubies throughout the entire land. The knights were bigger, stronger, and had greater weapons than the warriors. Many other warriors had tried before to defeat the knights, but all of them failed to win back the island. However, this chief warrior was different. He had a greater level of commitment. He recruited an army of warriors who were willing to fight for the island. He only wanted the troops who were decisive and didn't hesitate to join in on the mission. They ventured off to sea with 100 men on four ships and made their way to the shore of the island. Before initiating their attack, the chief warrior took a few days to strategize on their approach and how they would defeat the knights. Morning after morning, they'd all meet and the chief warrior would remind the troops of how great of fighters they were, what battles they had already won, and how they were going to take back the treasure-filled island. Then the day came. All of the troops had been anticipating this moment. Like many of the days before, they all met on the shore in front of the ships that they rode in on and gathered to hear the chief warrior's pre-fight speech. They were waiting for his words of encouragement and to receive instructions on their attack. Instead the chief warrior said something that changed everything for the entire army. What he said shifted the energy throughout each and every fighter. The chief warrior gave a command that shocked them all—*"Burn the ships!"* Many of the troops wondered how'd they get home if things didn't go as planned. How would they escape if they needed to retreat? The chief warrior responded, *"I'm a chief and chief's don't run. You are a warrior and warriors don't lower their standards to defeat. We will go back in their ships. Either we win or we fall trying!"* Each warrior now realized that their only option was success. They had come too far to back down now. It was at that moment that the soldiers became fully committed to victory, and with a smaller, less equipped army, the chief warrior led his fighters to victory.

The warriors weren't bigger in size, but they were bigger in commitment. They weren't the strongest in numbers but they were willing to risk it all. They burned off every ship of retreat and conquered. They made the decision to go for it and they did the impossible.

The question is, what ships do you need to burn that you find to be an easy escape from your dreams?—or that cause you to run away from challenges and miss out on your treasure? Are they excuses, fear, limitations, your past?

Burn the ships and commit. If you are going to be and do anything extraordinary in life, then you have to make the executive decision to pursue the dream that's calling you. You have to decide what you're going to value more, comfort or greatness, and be willing to eliminate any and all options of quitting.

Burn the ships and commit. Accept the responsibility and say yes to the calling on your life. It won't always be easy, but it will be worth it so take the risk of pursuing what makes you come alive. Give yourself permission to be great and to take action. When you persevere through self-doubt, fear, and procrastination, you'll experience new levels of self-discovery. The treasure you'll find is the one already on the inside of you. It's through pursuing our dreams that we find out who we really are and what we are truly made of. You can't wait for evidence that your dream will work to start making efforts towards achieving it...you'll never achieve the goals you never go after.

Burn the ships and commit. Will it feel like the *right* time? When fear is involved, it never will feel like the right time. You just have to make the decision to take action on what matters to you. Don't wait for someone to give you permission to begin. Don't wait for others to validate you. If God gave you the vision then you don't need to ask for permission. The stars don't have to be aligned. It doesn't have to be perfect just make sure its right and decide to go for it.

Burn the ships and commit.

DON'T BE ALARMED

YOUR HARDEST TIMES OFTEN LEAD TO THE GREATEST MOMENTS OF YOUR LIFE

There are many things we all sometimes dread. Being stuck in rush hour traffic, having to wait through ads on YouTube or Pandora, or receiving a group message where you're getting text notifications about things that have absolutely nothing to do with you. The list could go on and on, but one thing that so many people dread in the morning, is hearing the loud and often annoying sound of the alarm clock. It seems to always kick on during the most inconvenient times. You are deep in your sleep, comfortable in your bed, and enjoying a shared experience between you and your pillow. You're resting peacefully and out of nowhere an unexpected loud ring fills your room demanding your attention. It takes you away from what you thought was paradise and forces you to address its loud ring. You can either hit snooze and go back to sleep or you can accept its invitation to start your new day.

For years, like most people I would refer to this clock as the alarm clock. Then, I began to wonder...why do we consider it to be an alarm? Why do we have to be alarmed to start a new day that's full of new possibilities? Every day is an opportunity, so it would only make sense to think of it as more of an opportunity clock. It's really a wake up call to begin a new and emerging day. It's a signal that you get another start. The start of something new may be intimidating for some people but for others it's an open door to a fresh beginning. In this chapter, you'll discover how to navigate through the unexpected moments in life without being alarmed and how to turn setbacks into new opportunities.

Life is full of moments. There's moments that take your breath away and there's those moments that, like the alarm clock, will wake you up. They'll force you out of your sleep, or in other words your comfort zone, and interrupt what you once knew to be normal. You can either choose to view these moments as frightening experiences or you can interpret them as wake up calls to something greater. It's how you respond to these moments that truly determines who you are.

Some of life's best moments happen unexpectedly. They happen without notice and often catch you off guard. When I first came up with the idea to become a speaker, I had no idea what I was getting myself into. I just had a vision, a passion for my dream, and the willingness to go for it. One thing that I've learned about success is that it's not linear—it's sequential. It's a quest, it's a journey, its an adventure that doesn't always work out the way you plan it. When we initially start pursuing our goals, we come up with a picture of how we think everything will come together—how everything will fall in place and pan out. We think that we'll be running on a straight path with a smooth surface and the finish line will remain clear in sight. But in reality, it's the complete opposite. There are mountains you have to climb, valleys you have to crawl through, and droughts you have to survive. There are ups and downs, and at times that finish line that once was crystal clear in sight won't be as visible.

As I began my speaking journey I didn't know what to anticipate. Sometimes it's best that we don't know. If we knew all that we'd have to go through to get to where we want to be in life, many people would be too intimidated to start in the first place. The process of success often requires you to step into the unknown and it takes heart and boldness to take this step. However, when you do decide to take this courageous step towards what seems to be unknown, you'll find that there's genius in boldness. There's power in boldness. There's magic in boldness. We each owe it to ourselves to experience a bold life.

This speaking journey of mine began because of an alarming moment and a bold decision. At the time, I was trying to figure out how I could take my dream of speaking to a new level. I was still working the same job, but again, I was comfortably dissatisfied. So rather than complaining about my situation I decided to change it by going all in on my dream. I came up with a game plan for my future and how I wanted things to unfold. I created timelines and marked dates for things that I wanted to have done and for when I hoped to be in position to leave my job. I was trying to plan my work and work my plan, but unfortunately...or fortunately, whatever way you want to look at it, my plans were interrupted.

While at work one day the district manager called me into his office and informed me that I was no longer needed. I was laid off just like that. Quick, fast, and in a hurry—*"Thank you for your services, but we have decided to let you go."* For over eight years, I had worked for this company. Trying my best to be at my best. Working fifty-hour weeks and ten-hour days. I gave a lot of me to this job— my time, my energy, my dedication. Throughout those eight years, there wasn't a question as to whether I was a reliable and dedicated employee. I took pride in my work ethic so every day I saw to it that I was an asset to the organization. I'm not mentioning this to toot my horn, to play the victim, or to look for sympathy. I'm bringing this up to demonstrate that sometimes you can be doing everything right, but be in the wrong place.

I had been going back and forth about taking that bold step to pursue my dream. However, this job was a place of comfort for me. *"It's not what I want to do but at least I'm getting a check"*—is what I'd tell myself to justify why I wasn't moving with a sense of urgency towards my goal. I felt secure and thought I had everything under control, but I wasn't fulfilled with what I was doing knowing that there was more in me. It's important to understand that comfort is the enemy of your greatness. In order for you to step into something greater you have to cross the boundary lines of your comfort zone. In my case, I was pushed over those boundary lines.

Losing my job came out of nowhere. I couldn't predict it or see it coming. When it happened I was confused but at the same time I understood what was going on. I had a dream that was calling my name and every day the cry would get louder, but I was running away from what seemed unfamiliar to me—constantly overthinking my next move and failing to take action.

Ambition is worthless without action and when your actions aren't as big as your goals you end up in a perpetual state of putting your dreams off. Who knows how long I would have subjected myself to sacrificing my greater potential for temporary comfort before life sounded an alarm that woke me up. I understood that it was time for a new and greater chapter in my life.

When the unexpected alarms and interrupts your comfort, you can either hit the snooze button to continue sleeping on your potential or you can accept the invitation to start something new. I had already tried being unhappy and miserable—why not try something new? I took being laid off as a sign and realized that it was time to be bold and pursue what I believed I could do. I made up my mind that I was no longer going to do things that did not express my heart. I was going to figure out how to make my dreams work.

We all face moments that interrupt our plans and life as we know it. Maybe it's losing a job, an opportunity closing in your face, or something tragic happening on your journey towards your dream. Life can come at you fast and at times leave you weighed down by the unexpected, but remember it's not the weight that weighs you down...it's the way you carry it. It's not about what happens, as much as it's about how you respond. Because how you respond to life's struggles is what determines what you achieve, who you become, and where you end up in life.

Here are a few things to keep in mind when the unexpected interrupts you on your journey towards your dream.

EVERY LOSS IS NOT A LOSS... SOME ARE WINS IN DISGUISE

There are some things you lose in life that really aren't losses. For me, in losing my job there was more to gain than what I initially thought I lost. We don't really get to this level of understanding unless we have the right perspective. A lot of times when we experience setbacks, misfortune, or disappointments, our first reaction is to focus on what we lost. That's because we become so consumed emotionally by what happened and in some way feel violated or victimized—but what does this do? It puts you in a mental trap of focusing on everything that you believe is wrong with your situation instead of focusing on everything that's right about your situation and how it can be used to better your life. There's a hidden meaning behind everything that we face and go through. Even the worst of what we've been through can be used to bring out the best in our lives.

Opportunity will sometimes come disguised. It's like a present packaged in ugly wrapping paper, but inside is something valuable and amazing. Opportunity can appear in a different form or come from a different direction than what we initially expected. It doesn't always come from ideal situations or perfect scenarios. There's not always a yellow brick road that will lead you to your life changing opportunity. Opportunities are sometimes born from struggle. Abraham Lincoln initially lost his run for senator and became president of the United States two years later. Walt Disney was fired from a newspaper publisher because he *"lacked imagination and had no good ideas"*, and later launched the Disney empire. Opportunities can come disguised in the form of misfortune, temporary defeat, and moments of frustration. If you rely solely on your feelings and frustrations, you'll be easily fooled.

You have to keep in mind that life isn't happening to you, but in so many ways it's happening for you. It's your responsibility to figure out how to profit from your losses because there's always something to gain. Being laid off from my job gave me more time to grow and develop in the things that mattered most to me. I had to figure out how to make a living, but I had more time to invest in myself and in my future. Had I remained where I was, I possibly would have continued to delay going after my dream. Hearing the words, *"We no longer need you."*, was the end of one chapter of my life and the beginning of another. There were other things that needed me and other goals that I needed to accomplish. It marked the launch of my speaking career and the start of a new journey. I went from being unemployed to becoming an international speaker. Which demonstrated to me that your setbacks in life could end up becoming your setups for success. You have to find the hidden meaning in your challenge and understand that every loss is not a loss. Maybe you've been faced with some unforeseen setback. Maybe you've been sidetracked because of an unwanted surprise that you didn't see coming. Understand that sometimes the best hello to a new opportunity is a goodbye to an old situation.

TRUST THE PROCESS

This is so important that I'll repeat it again: Life is not happening to you, life is happening for you. Remember, life is not about the destination—it's more about the journey. Success is not something you do—it's something you become. Achievement doesn't just happen—it's a process that's made to happen. When we are met with challenges and face the unexpected, we tend to doubt the process and lose hope. When you lack hope, you'll find yourself feeling defeated, taking on the role of a victim, and feeling sorry for yourself. Having a *"woe is me"* attitude and believing that everyone and everything is out to get you will hinder you from moving your life forward.

You will never succeed at anything when you identify yourself as the victim—because you'll always be looking out the window to find something to blame, instead of looking in the mirror to better yourself.

The day that I was released from my job, I found myself trying to play the victim. I felt shame, I felt violated, and I was angry, but I soon realized that this way of thinking was not going to help me create a new future. You can't evaluate possibilities when your mind is stuck on problems. You don't move your life forward by fighting the old, you move forward by building the new. I decided that I wasn't going to feel sorry for myself and blame others but instead I was going to trust the process and start building my dreams. Even though apart of me wanted to think that being let go happened to me, I had to believe that it was happening for me. I was pushed out of my comfort zone, but I had to believe that it was for my benefit.

Trusting the process is all about rising above your situation. You have to find some level of peace in your discomfort. In the same way that an eagle flies above the clouds during a storm, you have to find a way to rise above your circumstance. Other birds take cover under the trees or they hide in different areas, but the eagle finds a way to elevate above the conditions. Which is why it gets to experience things that other birds can't.

There's two things that contribute to helping you find peace and maintain a positive attitude, especially while growing through your own personal process of success: Never losing hope and believing in yourself.

Hope is an acronym for *"HOLD ON PAIN ENDS"*. Life doesn't have to stay this way, it may be a struggle right now but things will get better. Not to say that things will get easier—but you will get stronger. What you go through, you'll grow through. You have to hold true that you can make it through your struggle and come out on top. Be totally convicted on the fact that you can survive the unexpected. Which leads to believing in yourself. Your daily language must be *I CAN DO THIS*. Believe that you can and will figure things out. Believe that you can handle what's thrown at you. Belief is like fuel to your fire. It will help you blaze a trail towards your dream.

The inspiring story of Chris Gardener chronicled in the movie starring Will Smith, *"The Pursuit to Happyness",* is a great example of trusting the process. He faced evictions, homelessness, jail, divorce, and many other unexpected challenges but eventually became a successful and wealthy stockbroker after growing through adversity. When you look at the individuals who came from nothing and achieved massive levels of success in life, it's because they held on to hope, believed in themselves, and trusted the process. When the unexpected happens it often comes with stress, worry, and anxiety, but when you trust the process you can overcome anything that you go through.

ATTITUDE IS KEY

There are some things that you just can't control—what other people think of you, what other's say to you, what others do, what happens around you—the economy, the weather, the future, gas prices, traffic, God's will...the list could go on and on. In fact, most of life you can't control, but in all truth...life is less about what happens and more about how you respond. What you can control is your attitude.

Having a positive attitude is one of the most important keys to success and having an overall great quality of life. Remember, you want to see every circumstance in your life as something that is happening for the best. This is how you'll see new possibilities that are available to you. Because even though some tragic or unfortunate things may occur, nothing is ever taken from you without being replaced by something of equal or greater value. Meaning your saddest, most frustrating experience can become your greatest asset in life if you maintain the right attitude. Contrary to this, if you adopt a negative attitude and keep your mind filled with thoughts of frustration and defeat, you will eventually attract those very things to you. You have to close your mind on all failures from your past. Not from the lessons you've learned from them, but from the pain that they have caused you.

My moments of loss or temporary defeat have taught me that what happens to you isn't what defeats you—it's your mental attitude toward it. Nothing or no one can hurt your feelings, make you angry, or upset you without your cooperation and consent. Never forget two beliefs that every successful person holds on to: They believe that tomorrow can and will be better than today, and they also firmly believe that they have the power to make it so. In essence, they have a positive outlook and attitude towards what they face.

The unexpected will push you out of your comfort zone and away from what you've been accustomed to, but it will also present to you new opportunities of growth, improvement, and advancement. You can only step into these opportunities when you have a positive attitude. A negative outlook won't give you access to these opportunities because a negative attitude is like a flat tire…you can't go anywhere until you change it.

When I was laid off, I asked myself, *"How can I align myself with my dream?"* I could have stressed about the challenges that lay ahead—and at first that was the direction that I wanted to go, but I instead, turned my problems into puzzles and with the right attitude I began to solve them.

A negative mind will never produce a positive life, so you have to keep your mind clear of any influence that doesn't promote positivity. It's important to understand that negative thoughts are weapons of mass destruction in your life, but enthusiasm and a positive attitude are weapons of mass creation. The right attitude can end up being stronger than any limitation. When I shifted my attitude from a negative state to a positive state, I was able to function effectively and was later able to find and create new opportunities that aligned with my dreams.

Through it all, you have control over your attitude. The choice is yours. You can choose to be positive or you can choose to be negative. You may not be able to effectively plan for, prepare for, or even prevent the unexpected, but if and when it occurs, the one thing that you have control over is you. When life happens, it can hit you when you think you're not ready, but in reality we each are equipped to handle whatever life throws at us. We can have a limited perspective of what we're capable of, but there are things that happen in life that help us realize that we are greater than what we even imagine. The unexpected can help align you with where you need to be. A setback can actually be setting you up for your dreams. You may lose something that you once thought was secure. Somebody may walk out of your life. There are many things that could happen, but remember that it's not happening to you…it's happening for you. If it was meant to be it will be, but your responsibility is learning and figuring out how you can turn an unexpected loss into a unanimous win.

They say hindsight is 20/20 and looking back, losing my job was one of the best things that happened to me. I had a dream and vision that excited me, but I was too uncertain to act on my own. I put it off for so long because I wanted to have everything figured out before I even took the first step. While I was trying to figure things out, life was moving and it wasn't going to wait on me. Life moves at its own pace. The unexpected will happen. Events will occur in our lives without our permission. It's not a matter of if, but when, and when you are faced with it, realize that every loss is not a loss, trust the process, and keep a positive attitude through it all. It's our job to convert trials into moments of triumph. You may be pushed out of your comfort zone and things can seem intimidating at times, but you have to focus your energy and efforts on things that contribute to your growth—because growth is truly what it's all about.

When a baby eagle reaches a certain size and maturity, life as he knows it begins to change. The father eagle realizes the eaglet's current growth as well as its potential for more growth. When the time is right the father eagle hovers over the nest where the eaglet lays comfortably. Being lifted by the breeze in midair, it spreads its wings to demonstrate to the eaglet that it could use its wings to lift itself out of the nest. Eagles were meant to fly, but at birth they don't initially know this…they have to be taught how to fly. If it were left up to the eaglet, they would stay within the comfort of the nest that it's used to. Knowing this, the father comes down into the nest and puts its head up against the eaglet and pushes it closer and closer to the edge of the nest. Until finally, he pushes the eaglet completely out of the nest, and the little one falls down the tree, sinking in the sky and heading towards the ground below. But the father flies down under the eaglet, catches it midair and takes the little one back up to the nest. It does this over and over again until the eaglet discovers that it has functional wings. The father does this because it knows that the little one was made to fly. The eaglet doesn't realize this, but the father pushes it out of the nest for it to realize what it's capable of. When the eagle feels that the little one is getting a sense of how to use its wings, it solidifies this learning moment by forcing the eaglet to create a new normal. The father goes back to the nest and removes the feathers inside, which symbolize comfort to the eaglet. He then goes to the edge of the nest and begins to tear the nest down, removing stick after stick. The eaglet looks on lost and confused, but the father eagle knows exactly what it's doing. He knows that as long as the eaglet relies on the nest, it will never fly...and now that the nest is gone, the eaglet is forced to spread the wings it was given and fly.

Don't be alarmed when dealing with the unexpected, because in many ways you are the eagle that must spread its wings and fly.

GROWTH
IS A LIFESTYLE

EVERY NEW DAY PROVIDES YOU WITH AN OPPORTUNTIY
TO EVOLVE INTO A GREATER VERSION OF YOU

There are two types of people—those who *want* to win and those who *train* to win. There are those that talk about where they want to go and those that actually put forth the effort. It's those that grow daily and become serious about their goals that become the ones that actually achieve them. In this chapter, you'll discover how developing a growth mindset can set you up for achievement and the one thing that you can do that is guaranteed to set you up for success.

If you know anything about trees, you know that you need patience after planting them because they take time to reach their full potential. One tree in particular, the Chinese Bamboo tree, takes exceptionally longer to reach its full potential. You start with a seed—plant it, and water it for an entire year—but nothing happens in that first year. In the second year you continue to water it...but again, nothing happens. The third year comes along and you keep watering, but still after all of your effort there is nothing to show for it. In the fourth year, you tend to the seed even more, but after another year of nurturing and watering the tree still doesn't develop. Four years goes by and nothing changes since planting the seed. Keep watering it because in the fifth year something different happens.

Your diligence and consistency pays off when the tree finally sprouts and grows ninety feet in a matter of six weeks.

Did the tree grow in six weeks or did it take a five-year process of nurturing to sprout out of the ground? It was the five-year process that prepared it for the six-week growth. The improvement process is a lot like the Chinese Bamboo Tree. It can get discouraging at times. There's times when it seems like you're not making any progress, but if you stay consistent, remain diligent, and continue to persist—even when you don't see the results—then, at some point your opportunity will present itself and amazing things can take place.

You can't just wish for it, you have to work for it. Any new level of achievement requires effort to get there. There are plenty of people that want to be more and achieve more, but only a few are willing to do more. There's plenty of people that want to be fit and in shape, but not everybody stays disciplined to monitor their diet and consistently work out. There are many people that want to turn their ideas into a business, but not everybody is willing to make the sacrifices and put forth the effort to become a successful entrepreneur. We come up with excuses—*It's too difficult. I don't really have the time for it. I would, but…*The thought of achieving the goal becomes overshadowed by what's involved in getting it done. In other words, some people's excuses become bigger than their goals so they avoid things that require effort. Why? Our natural tendency as people is to seek comfort and avoid pain. So we naturally want to steer away from anything that pushes us out of our comfort zone. This is a conflict that we all deal with, but to get to where you want to be in life, you have to do what is necessary.

There are two types of people, those that are satisfied by pleasing methods and those that are satisfied by pleasing results. The ones that are satisfied by pleasing results do what's necessary and they create the results they want…while the ones that are satisfied by pleasing methods are forced to accept whatever they get because of their lack of effort. Understanding this, you must realize that in order to get ahead in life, you have to go against your human conditioning to stick with what's comfortable and be willing to do the things that stretch you—clocking in on your dreams even when you don't feel like it. Investing time and energy on your craft, even when you're frustrated. Working diligently to improve even when you're discouraged. Growth has to be a way of life if you want to build your dreams.

BECOME WHAT YOU WANT

Every master, at some point, was once a disaster. Every professional was once an amateur. Everybody starts somewhere. Contradictory to popular belief, greatness isn't something that you're just born with...it's something that you have to develop. When I first began public speaking, I knew I had to get better at delivering a message. To be a professional you have to perform like one. I made a commitment to improve. I started attending Toastmasters meetings. I started speaking in front of small groups. During conversations, I'd work on getting better. Any chance I could get, I would find a way to improve. As a way to work on my skills as a speaker and to share my message, I started recording and uploading videos to social media. To say that speaking in front of a camera was a struggle for me is an understatement. It was extremely challenging. It would take me hours to record a video that was only a few minutes long. I would stumble over my words, forget what I wanted to say, and freeze in front of the camera. I would overthink what I was doing, what I was saying, and how I was saying it. It was such a challenge because I was forcing myself out of my comfort zone. There were many times I'd get frustrated, discouraged, and would even wonder if all the effort was even worth it. However, in spite of my frustration, I was growing through it all.

Practice makes progress and diligence creates excellence. Growth is a process and any type of process that produces something great takes time. There's going to be some rocky stages, but if you keep at it and stay consistent, you'll eventually improve. At the time, I couldn't see how those frustrating moments were helping me improve. I couldn't see how the countless hours I initially thought were being wasted were helping me develop my craft as a speaker and strengthening my confidence. In anything, repetition is what produces skill, so with every attempt, I was getting better.

If you ever want to be taken serious at anything...be consistent. Every day I would show up and continue to post videos on social media. I let go of the thought of trying to be perfect and instead looked at each video and each speech as a way to impact lives and grow in my field. Consistency is what draws attention and I soon started to notice my efforts paying off. One of those people who noticed my message was an event planner that happened to be planning an event that they wanted me to be the keynote speaker for. The amazing thing about this event was that it was actually a live televised event that had nearly 1,000 attendees and tens of thousands of viewers. Being that I was just starting as a speaker, I knew that this opportunity was not only a blessing but also a testament to how diligence can open up doors. It was because I was willing to do what at first was uncomfortable and remain committed to growth, that I was able to attract opportunities that were aligned with where I wanted to be. In life, we don't attract the things that we want, we only attract the things that we are. I became a speaker. I didn't wait for the stage or to have a microphone in my hand. I started to do what I wanted to do wherever I found myself. On the internet, at the grocery store, at a basketball game—it didn't matter where I was. I used each moment as an opportunity to inspire and encourage others. I became what I wanted for my life. As I continued to invest in myself and continued to become more of what I wanted, opportunities began to open up. It just goes to show that anything worth doing is worth doing poorly while you learn to do it well.

You become the things that you want by practice, repetition, and incorporating them into your daily behavior. In doing this, you'll start to attract the opportunities that are associated with your goals. You can't expect to achieve million dollar dreams with a minimum wage work ethic. Your work ethic has to represent where you want to take your life. Your mindset, decisions, and daily habits have to match the goal that you've set for yourself.

COMPETENCE AND CONFIDENCE

Moment by moment and day by day, get better and better in every single way— look at every day as an opportunity to scale up and get better. There is no top ceiling to achievement, but each ceiling of achievement that you jump through will become the floor to your next level. Developing a mindset of growth can have a tremendous positive influence.

What you believe is what shapes what you achieve. When you believe in growth, diligence, and mastery, you set the stage for improving as a person and accomplishing your dreams. What you believe about your abilities will help determine how you interpret your life experience and will eventually set the boundaries on what you'll set out to accomplish. If you believe that your potential, abilities, and skills are fixed, then you will set up limitations and restrictions for yourself. Which will cause you to shut down new ideas and reject new opportunities. However, if you believe that your knowledge, skills, and abilities are areas that you can develop, then you'll open your life up to the exciting world of possibilities.

I never would have imagined that I could develop the skill to speak in front of people. I figured that speaking was something that I just couldn't do. My mind was fixed on the false belief that I could not grow as a speaker, but when I became open to growth in that area it changed my life forever. When you narrow it down, the two things that separate you from who you are now and who you can become, are confidence and competence. To reach new levels of achievement you have to believe in yourself and you have to be confident in what you can accomplish. Seeking growth will immerse you in experiences that help you develop in both these areas.

Competence is tied to your access to information, knowledge, and how you actively apply what you've learned. As the old wise saying goes—*"When you know better, you do better."*

Confidence is connected to your mindset, skills, capabilities, and experiences. Developing a positive attitude, improving your skills, and participating in experiences that challenge you, will help you become a more confident person. Whenever we find ourselves being doubtful or intimidated by some type of challenge, it's because we lack connection with one or more of these aspects of confidence. When you feel you lack the skills, it affects your confidence. When you believe that you're not qualified, this belief will begin to reflect in your confidence. This lack of connection has a great influence on the way you view what you're capable of achieving. Identifying what you're lacking is the first step to strengthening your confidence. *Ask yourself*: What information do I need to learn to become more competent? What do I need to connect with to be more confident? What skills do I need to develop? What false beliefs do I need to eliminate to make way for more confidence?

This is all apart of growth. The time you invest in yourself is what determines how you operate your life, how far you take your goals, and what dreams you achieve. If you sketch and draw every day, you'll eventually get better at it. If you talked in front of a group of people every week, your confidence will become greater than your fear of pubic speaking. If you write an article every week, you'll soon be more competent as an author. When you do something every day that scares you or that's challenging, the result is growth.

THE DIFFERENCE MAKER

Achievement is the sum of daily efforts repeated day in and day out. This requires effort, which is what many people run away from. Thomas Edison once said, *"Opportunity is missed by most people because it's dressed in overalls and looks like work."* Don't fall into this trap. You have to be different. The average person wants to do what's easy and take the path of least resistance, but the easy road will limit your life.

Why is it that some people succeed at their goals while others don't? Why is it that there are some people that seem to win at everything they attempt while there are others that can't seem to win at anything at all? A part of me used to think that it was all about your upbringing, but then I began to learn about people like Oprah Winfrey who had been abused as a child. Despite her early struggles she became one of the most influential women on the planet. Then part of me used to assume that maybe age had a lot to do with it. I thought you had to wait until you were a certain age and if you were past that age it was too late. Then I started discovering stories like the one of Moziah Bridges who started a successful bow tie business in Memphis, Tennessee at the age of 9, and Colonel Sanders who founded KFC in his senior years. I also used to think that success depended on your talent level. Until I noticed that there were many talented people that were missing success because they weren't doing anything with their abilities. I went on and on about what I thought was the deciding factor as to why some people succeed while others don't, but everything pointed back to one simple reason. It's a simple concept to understand but at times it's difficult to apply. However, I do believe that if you could put this concept into practice in your life, there's nothing that you can't do. The key difference that separates those that achieve their goals and those that fall short, is simply that the individuals that succeed are willing to do the things that others won't do. They make a daily decision to go above and beyond and do the things that others aren't willing to do. They create *"non-negotiables"* and have a *"no excuses"* mentality to get to where they want to be in life.

The work that many people reject, is the work that the achievers choose to do. When others are seeking comfort, they realize that they have to do what's uncomfortable to get to where they want to be. They are the first ones there and the last to leave. They stop when the job is done, not when time expires. They don't procrastinate on what's important. They act with a sense of urgency and are led by the realization that opportunities don't last forever. They go the extra mile to achieve their goals. There are days when they don't feel like doing the work, but they do the work anyway because of the results that they want to create. The average person seeks pleasing methods, while the achievers seek pleasing results. They do what's required and eventually become satisfied with the outcomes their efforts create.

It all boils down to how committed you are to your goals. Are you willing to show up for your dreams?—and not just every once in a while, but every single day. We all have our share of challenges that we face as we build a better life, but to leave a mark in this world you have to become a master of yourself and stay disciplined to work towards your dreams.

Take 5-time NBA Champion Kobe Bryant for example, who when asked how athletes improve he said, *"Great things come from hard work and perseverance. You have to have a no excuses mentality"* Kobe faced many challenges in his career—injuries, tough losses, disagreements with teammates, just to name a few...but through it all he stayed committed to growth. When other players were sleeping, he was developing his handles. While other players were taking time off, he was mastering his jump shot. Other players would arrive to practice late, while Kobe was there hours before schedule. That's why he was a force to be reckoned with and well respected on the court. That's why he is a Hall of Fame caliber athlete. That's why he will go down as one of the best to do it—not just because of his skill and talent, but because of his willingness to do what others weren't willing to do.

You may not be a star athlete, but you are talented in one area or another. There's some amazing work that you are capable of creating. It's important to understand that whatever you're aiming for in life, become the *best you at it*. Work to be the best you can possibly be. Your only competition is the person you were 24 hours ago. Every day, be wiser, smarter, stronger, more skilled, and better than that person. This requires a daily effort and discipline to push yourself to the next level. You have to be willing to sacrifice who you are now for who you can become.

You have to leave your old ways and embrace new approaches. View your challenges from a different perspective and persist through the difficulties of growth. Don't be afraid to work. Your dream, your goal, your life's calling comes with a price. Be willing to pay the price by any means necessary. Many people come up with countless reasons why they aren't where they want to be, but excuses will never lead you to achievement. Don't be controlled by them. Move beyond them. Get rid of them. When your dreams become bigger than your excuses you'll give birth to success.

STRUCTURE YOUR LIFE AROUND YOUR GOAL

The future belongs to those that seek out ways to better themselves. You do this by organizing your life in a way that will help you achieve the results that you're aiming for. Start by setting the priority of what's important to you. What are you aiming to accomplish? What really matters to you? Think about what area in your life you'd like to experience significant improvement in and make that a priority. Once you have this priority established, structure your days around developing in this area. If you want to be a better artist, set aside time every day to work on your craft. If you want to grow in your business, devote your energy towards learning more about your industry. If your goal is to be a better photographer, invest time every day to get better at taking photos.

One of the most successful comedians, Jerry Seinfeld, understood the importance of structuring your life around a goal. When asked how to become a great comic Seinfeld answered by saying, *"The way to be a better comic was to create better jokes and the way to create better jokes was to write every day."*

Seinfeld had a calendar system he used to pressure himself to write. He'd grab a calendar and a big red marker and would mark "X" over each day he wrote a joke. *"After a few days you'll have a chain. Keep at it and the chain will grow longer every day. Your only job is to not break the chain."*

Don't break the chain. That's your job. Don't stop growing. Don't stop improving. Don't break the chain. Daily action is what builds extraordinary results. When you structure your time in ways that allow you to invest in your knowledge, skills, and abilities, you'll create a successful rhythm. In other words, you'll create successful habits that move you towards your ultimate goal. It's your habits that truly determine the results that you create and ultimately the kind of life you live. What you do every day is far more important than what you do every once in a while. A dancer can practice their routine for an hour one day out of the week, but that won't guarantee that they'll get the audition when there are others that are practicing for hours every single day. A student can study the night before an exam and hope to do well the next day, but they'd be better off taking time out every day to learn their coursework. We are creatures of habit, but we want to become masters of habits. You want to put yourself in a position where it is nearly impossible for you to fail because you've mastered the skills necessary to take advantage of your opportunity. You do this by structuring your life around growth and establishing successful habits.

The majority of habits that lead you towards success actually require no talent at all. They just require discipline—maintaining a good attitude, being willing to learn, making sound decisions, having a strong work ethic, being prepared, showing up each day ready to go the extra mile and go all in on your goals—these are all daily decisions that you have to discipline yourself to make. Not only does growth require discipline, but it also requires dedication. Your dreams should be demonstrated in your daily behavior. Actions speak louder than words, tweets, Facebook statuses, and Instagram posts. The grind has to be more than just a hashtag. You don't want to just look successful through screens and filters, you want to be successful in life. Your day-by-day actions should demonstrate that you are building something better for your life. Remember, the average person wants to do what's easy, but the easy road doesn't lead to greatness. Be willing to do the things that others won't and your efforts will build your dreams. It would be a misfortune to value something and have a passion for some goal, but never commit to putting forth your best effort towards achieving it. In life, you ask for what you want, but you pay for what you get. You pay with your efforts, and only you can determine what level of effort you are going to put forth in order to grow and become a greater you. Organize your life around your goal, structure your days around what's important to you, stay dedicated and you'll eventually find your way to achievement.

Will you have to make sacrifices? Yes, you may miss out on things—while others are sleeping on their dreams you have to be up building yours. While others are having a good time during happy hour, you have to keep your focus on building a great life. There are going to be days when it gets hard to continue to work on a vision that at times only you will see, but be patient, remain confident, and stay hungry. Growth is never easy, but learn from your failures, make adjustments after every mistake, and approach each day with the understanding that you haven't given your best yet. Keep growing into your best. This is the call of duty for high achievement. It's a call that comes with great responsibility. It's a call that will test your commitment and dedication to your dreams. It's a call that will often frustrate and discourage you, but you can't have the good without the bad. They aren't sold separately. You have to take it with a grain of salt and do what you have to do to get to where you want to be—because on the flip side, this call will lead you to achievement. It will lead you down the path of success and fulfillment. It will help you live out your destiny and become everything that you potentially can be.

Remember, the achievers succeed because they are willing to do the things that others won't. Colonel Sanders was rejected 1000 times for his KFC recipe, and now there are nearly 19,000 locations in over 100 countries. Michael Phelps trained 7 days a week, 365 days a year, from the time he was 14 years old until the Beijing Olympics. Which is why he's one of the greatest Olympians of all time. Kevin Hart was booed off stages early in his career, but he stuck with it and made adjustments and now has become iconic in the world of comedy. The founders of Pandora approached 300 investors while constantly improving their product before getting funding for their startup, and the company is now worth billions of dollars. With any story of achievement, one common thread that you'll find is a commitment to growth and the willingness to find a way to achieve.

Like the Chinese Bamboo Tree, for you to see growth and results it takes effort, patience, and consistency. If you slack up and don't water your dream, you may miss your opportunity. It may take longer than you initially expected, but if you stay committed, your results can astonish you. Whatever you want for your life, be willing to do what others aren't and you'll be able to experience a life that others can't. Through the frustrations of growth and the delayed gratification, make daily efforts and take daily steps to build your dreams. Big opportunities are created by small consistent efforts. Build the momentum of growth and you'll become a force to be reckoned with. Make growth your lifestyle.

UNSTOPPABLE

YOU BECOME UNSTOPPABLE THE MOMENT YOU
COMMIT TO NEVER GIVING UP

B eing unstoppable isn't just about your skills, abilities, or even about how talented and experienced you are. It has more to do with your state of mind. No one is exempt from the challenges that come with pursuing goals, yet you may ask how some are able to overcome these obstacles and win despite their challenges? It's because they are led by an unstoppable mindset. The winners keep moving forward despite what they feel and keep rising despite what they experience. In this chapter, you'll discover how to stay determined, how to persist through adversity, and how to achieve your goals in life.

In the jungle, which animal is the biggest? The elephant. Which animal is the tallest? The giraffe. Which animal is the wisest? The serpent. Which animal is the fastest? The cheetah. Out of these categories, the lion is never mentioned. Why then is the lion considered to be the *"King of the Jungle"*?

The lion isn't the biggest, the fastest, or the smartest... Why does the lion get so much respect? It's because of the lion's unstoppable mindset.

The lion is known to have a fighting mentality and an unrelenting approach to dominating its territory. At the age of two, the male lions are forced out of their pride to venture off and start their own. Which is when the fighting begins. The lion has to learn how to provide for itself and eventually start its own pride. So, from the age of two, the lion is constantly fighting to own territory and to take control of a pride. Only the strong lions survive.

Because the lion grows up engaged in battle, it develops a level of courage and confidence that is unmatched by no other animal. This is why it's the *"King of the Jungle"*. With its fighting mindset and relentless attitude, the lion dominates any and everything that stands in front of what it wants. It walks with confidence even while constantly being tested by other animals. It never backs down. The lion is bold, fearless, and always ready to face any challenge because it believes it's unstoppable.

Like the lion you will have to fight for the territory of your dreams. Great things don't come easy. In the words of Frederick Douglas, *"If there is no struggle, there will be no progress."* Adversity is apart of the journey to success. It's the ultimate test of ones' character. Times of challenge and controversy are what reveal what you're really made of. As you pursue your big dreams in life, there will be times when your hope and faith are questioned. The possibility of your goals may be unclear at times and there will be moments when you even question your belief in yourself. Instead of backing down when things get challenging, or giving up when things become difficult, you have to maintain the same unstoppable mindset as the lion. You have to fight for your success and protect your dreams.

DON'T DO WHAT MOST PEOPLE DO

It's easy to be motivated when you see results, but what do you do when it seems like your efforts aren't paying off? It's easy to stay positive when everything is going right, but what do you do when it seems like everything is falling apart around you? It's exciting to work toward your dreams when you see the fruits of your labor, but what do you do when the outcomes aren't what you expected? The journey of achievement has its ups and downs and the challenges of success will sometimes use your enthusiasm against you.

When you start working towards your goal—you're motivated to move forward, inspired to improve your life, and ready to experience more. As much as we hate to face it, things don't always go as planned. Things may not happen as fast as we hoped. The road to success won't always be smooth and in many cases your excitement can fold into frustration. Your ambition can turn into neglect and carelessness. Your drive can get placed in park and what was once a definite dream, can turn into a farfetched fantasy. Leaving you wondering, *"Is it even possible?"*, *"Can I really do this?"*, or *"Will it ever happen?"*.

Most people fail to finish when things get rough. When their dreams seem to be more than what they bargained for, they throw in the towel and give up short of their goal. There's an urge to quit, and they give in. Spending their entire lives quitting on things when they get hard. They start pursuing their goals only to stop when the effort becomes challenging. They begin with high hopes, but end with frustrating defeats. Going from one thing to the next, but never reaching their true potential because they give up too soon.

Success comes with some form of resistance and the journey will get difficult at times, but don't be like most people. Don't approach your dreams like the average person. Be different and overcome the urge to quit.

A LESSON IN THE CLASSROOM OF ADVERSITY

Mike Tyson once said, *"Everybody has a plan until they get punched in the face."* You may come up with the best strategic approach or the greatest plan to achieve your goal, but adversity has a way of throwing you off course.

When I started competing as a boxer I quickly learned one key lesson—the sport is more about your mental toughness than it is about your physical strength. You can be the biggest and the strongest, but if your mind isn't disciplined to battle through the intensity of a fight, you'll get defeated. When you see two fighters going toe to toe in the ring, the one that keeps their mental composure is typically the one that becomes victorious. Of course, skill and ability have a lot to do with it, but overall your mental strength plays a huge role. You train your mind to overcome anxious nerves because if your muscles are tight, then your timing suffers. You condition your mind to stay poised and not get angry when you get hit because when angry, your emotions take over your ability to make sound decisions—which could cost you tremendously. There are times when you get hit by a good and well-timed punch that can throw you off, but you have to push past the pain if you want the victory. Overall, it's not just your opponent that stands in your way of becoming a champion, but in many ways, you're in competition with yourself. It's more about you getting out of your own way and staying single-minded to win.

Boxing is symbolic to the adversity that life can sometimes hand us. It's a great representation of the journey of achievement and how we get hit by challenges. Life will hit you with a good shot that can leave you confused. Moments of defeat can knock the wind out of you. Setbacks can buckle your knees and failure will leave you slumped on the canvas of life. There are those moments that will have you debating whether you should continue fighting or throw in the towel. They leave you wondering if you even have what it takes to succeed. In life, just like a fighter inside the ring, you have to discipline your mind to stay focused on winning—you have to remain poised to withstand challenges, roll with the punches, and continue to fight for your victory.

Who would Rocky be if he didn't have to fight Ivan Drago or Apollo Creed? Would Michael Jordan have been as great if he didn't get cut from his high school basketball team? The challenges that we face can fuel us to optimize our potential. As much as you may despise it, adversity is your greatest teacher. Every defeat, every loss, every heartbreak comes with a lesson. Difficult experiences come with life improving lessons. That's why you should never look at your challenges as a disadvantage. They may seem to be inconvenient, but you'll soon find out that there's strength to be found in your struggle. The challenges along your journey bring out the best in you. They develop your character, and like Martin Luther King Jr. said, *"The ultimate measure of a man is not where he stands in moments of comfort and convenience, but where he stands at times of challenge and controversy."* How you respond to adversity will determine how you live your life. You can be defined by your struggles or the process of pushing through them can build you.

Anything worthwhile has a process to endure before it can reach its full potential. Gold has to be thrown in the fire before it shines. Diamonds have to be cut before they sparkle. Butterflies have to be isolated in a cocoon before they get wings. The process is what transforms one thing into another. Success is a process, and as much as you want to at times, you can't skip it. Every part of you will be tested while you're pressing towards your dreams, but don't allow discouragement to take you to a place of defeat in your mind. It's when you are defeated in your mind that you'll be defeated by life. Stay strong and realize that tough times won't last, but tough people do. The hard times show you what you're made of. It's in the process that you discover more about yourself and transform into a greater person. No matter how tough things get, you have to be like the lion and hold an unstoppable mindset.

THE UNSTOPPABLE MINDSET: COMMITMENT

How do you develop an unstoppable mindset? You first have to realize that you'll never conquer something you're not committed to. In other words, decide what you want for your life and commit to making it happen. In this fast paced, immediate, and "*want everything instantly*" world, we too often assume that great things will happen overnight. Google can answer any question you have instantly. You can stream any movie you want at a moment's notice. Fast food restaurants will prepare your meal in a matter of seconds. We expect instant gratification, microwave success, and drive-thru breakthroughs, but this is not the case when it comes to achieving your goals. The process of success takes time. Giving birth to your dreams may take longer than you initially expect. On top of that, the plans that you create may not go as smooth as you anticipate. There may be things that arise that you aren't fully prepared for. What do you do then? Do you give up on everything that you've dreamed of? Not at all! You have to be committed.

Like many college students, it took me longer than four years to graduate with my Bachelors. In fact, it took me six years to get a four-year degree. There were many challenges that stood in my way, but because I made the commitment to graduate, I didn't let anything stop me.

I started in community college after being rejected by every university I applied for. I didn't know much about how to get through college. My parents never attended college and I didn't know very many people who had pursued higher education. I had no scholarships and didn't qualify for financial aid. I had heard many horror stories about how students were graduating with the crushing weight of student loan debt, and I decided that I didn't want that…so I picked up a full-time job to pay for tuition. On top of that, I was competing with USA Boxing, which set the stage for years of discipline in my life. I was a full time student, a full time employee, and a competing athlete—my focus was on bettering my future. Every day I had to stay disciplined to study for classes, train for fights, and work to pay bills and tuition. There were late nights preparing for exams, early morning training sessions, and long ten-hour shifts at work. Work, training, school...work, training, school...this became my daily routine seemed to pack all my days together. There were times when I felt I had been in college for too long and wasn't making progress. There were periods when I would get frustrated because I was working fifty-hour workweeks, and would dish out all my money on tuition and expensive textbooks. There were moments when I would go to sleep tired, wake up tired, and had to push myself through the day. It wasn't easy, but I was making a sacrifice to set up my future.

I'd be lying to you if I told you that I didn't get discouraged from time to time. It wouldn't be true if I said that there weren't moments that I felt like quitting. But when I was tired—I stayed committed. When I got discouraged—I stayed committed. When I felt like giving up—I stayed committed. I was committed to my goal and what could be instead of allowing my feelings to talk me into quitting. My father always taught me, *"Don't start something that you can't finish"*. So, I knew that since I started this journey of graduating from college, I had to be committed no matter what and finish the journey...and I did just that. After six years, I walked across the stage at graduation and became a first generation college graduate with no debt to my name. All because I stayed committed.

The race is not given to the swift, nor the strong, but to those that can endure and keep pressing on. Being committed is staying loyal to what you said you were going to do, long after the mood you had when you said it is gone. When the initial thrill is gone, you have to stick with it. When the struggle is real, you have to hang in there. When your back is up against the wall, you have to keep moving forward. Commitment is what fuels perseverance and discipline. When you make it your responsibility to achieve your goals, you'll find a way to succeed.

The truth is that no goal can have a great effect on your life unless you take it seriously—unless you're fully invested. Many people flirt with their dreams. They just toy with the idea of venturing towards something greater. Some people only date their dreams, pursuing their goals only when it's convenient. But if you're going to make any transformational success happen in your life, you have to be fully committed to your dreams. No if's, and's, or but's...you have to go all in on what you want.

If you don't commit to something, you'll be distracted by everything, and these distractions can destroy your chances of optimizing your life.

Commit to your own growth and expansion. Commit to your truth, your future, and to bettering your life. Commit to improving life for your family and for the world you live in. Be more committed to your goals and dreams than you are to your doubts and fears. Stay committed to taking risks, evolving as a person, and being true to you. Make a commitment to your visions and dreams. Take a stand for your deepest values and beliefs. Pledge to do everything it takes to live by them. Don't let your obstacles stop you. Don't allow the struggle to keep you down. When most people are met by challenges, they run from one thing to the next trying to find the easy road. There is no easy road to success. Commit to doing whatever's necessary to get where you want to be in life.

You owe it to yourself to commit to becoming the greatest you. The world is full of many talented people who are proficient, skilled, and capable of achieving amazing things, but because they lack the drive and the willingness to commit to their dreams, they fail to make meaningful progress in life. They start but never finish, and their future suffers because they constantly find themselves giving up. The unstoppable ones are the ones that are the most committed. Kill the cycle of quitting, stick to your vision, and find a way to move forward.

THE UNSTOPPABLE MINDSET: DETERMINATION

It's not just wanting to win that makes you a winner. Winners are the ones that refuse to fail. To be unstoppable, you have to be determined. Determination is made up of having the burning desire to win and a total refusal to fail.

Winning starts in the mind. It's an attitude. When Serena Williams steps on the court, she's thinking about winning. When Mark Cuban is about to close a deal, he's thinking about winning. Winning has to be a constant thought that runs through your mind if you are going to be unstoppable. Even when the circumstances seem stacked against you, you have to focus on the outcomes you want, instead of the circumstances you see. Don't allow your current circumstances to limit your long-term vision. You're going to make mistakes. You will fail at times, but remember that it's impossible to beat someone who never gives up. By refusing to fail, you set yourself up for success. It may not happen instantly, but eventually you'll find a way.

When adversity rises, you have to rise above it and keep your mind set on winning.

No matter how many times you fall…keep rising. Reject any form of settling, put yourself in position to learn from your mistakes, and grow from your circumstances.

Sports taught me a lot about determination. One of the big tournaments in boxing is the Golden Gloves. It's the tournament to win. I would train hard knowing that the tournament was coming—running for miles, spending hours strength training, hitting the bags, mitt work, sparring, and doing countless sit-ups. However, after all the hard work I put in, I still came up short during this tournament. Depending on how many fighters were in your weight class, you had to fight every week, sometimes up to six consecutive weeks. You had to weigh in before each fight and couldn't be an ounce overweight. To advance to the next round, you had to either stop your opponent or out point them in the decision.

The first year I competed in the tournament, I was outpointed. The second year, I made it to the quarterfinals and lost on points. The third year, I made it to the semifinals and fell short again. Imagine the feeling. I would sacrifice my time training and focusing on getting better as a boxer. I disciplined myself to be consistent with the right diet. I would work hard in the gym and trained to win, but would still fall short. These were frustrating and upsetting moments. At times, my impatience would get the best of me, but I kept coming back to fight. The fourth year, I made it to the semifinals again, but like the previous year…I came up short.

Another year, another shortcoming. Another try and another failure. Nobody likes to lose. It's disappointing, and when you've been working at something for so long, it can be devastating to fall short. For this to be the fourth time in a row, it was disheartening. How did I really feel? I felt like I was letting my trainer down, like I was letting my supporters down, and more importantly, like I was letting myself down. I knew that I could win this tournament. I knew that I could be #1. What made it even tougher to deal with, was the fact that I was losing by a small number of points. One point here or two points there. If I had done just a little more during the fight then I would've had my hand raised in the end. But in the fifth year, my mindset was different. Not to say that I wasn't focused before, but I was on another level of focus. This time around I trained like never before, and my mind wasn't just focused on winning. I reached the point where I refused to fail. I wasn't going to beat myself. I wasn't going to cheat myself. I wasn't even going to leave the fight in the hands of the judges. I was going to make it crystal clear that I was the winner. I fought every week for five weeks straight leading up to the championship bout. I was in the zone, dominating every bout and raising my hand in victory after every match. Then the night of the finals, I began to think about the journey leading up to this point—the years I had came up short, the hard work that I invested in the gym, the disappointments and the pain that I felt after losing. Stepping into the ring, I was a man on a mission. I wasn't about to let anybody take this moment away from me—not my opponent, not the judges, and not even myself. Halfway during the second round, the referee stopped the fight, after I knocked my opponent down. Refusing to fail paved the way for me to win.

That journey taught me so much about perseverance and determination. Not only how it could be used in the boxing ring, but more importantly, how it could be used in life. There are some things that will never come easy. There are some goals that will come with resistance. At times, your dreams may seem impossible, but if you can sustain the initial motivation that you had when you started, continue to give the same level of effort when things get rough, remember why you started in the first place, and never forget that your time is coming—there will be no limits to what you can achieve. That's determination. That's how you win. That's being unstoppable.

One of my favorite lines from the *Rocky* series is, "*It aint about how hard you hit, it's about how hard you can get hit and keep moving forward. It's about how much you can take, and keep moving forward. That's how winning is done.*" If you can keep moving forward, you can win. If you can keep moving forward, you can succeed. It's the ones that are determined that win. It's the ones that never back down that achieve the impossible. The ones that refuse to fail are the ones that accomplish their dreams.

Oaks grow strong in contrary winds, rough waters develop skilled sailors, and adversity is meant to help you grow in life. Don't let it stop you from living your life. The challenges that we wrestle will strengthen our character and sharpen our skills. Rivers are able to cut through rocks, not because of the power of the water, but because of their persistence. The amazing thing about determination is that it is always followed by a breakthrough. Breakthroughs happen when you don't give up. If you want to breakthrough to your next level...believe you are unstoppable. Remember, it starts in your mind. In the same way the lion owns its territory, you have to own your mind. Don't allow your challenges to shift your attention away from what's important. Manage the stress when things get overwhelming. Override any impulses and thoughts of quitting. Own your mind and be just as determined as the lion to own your life.

Success is not a sprint, it's a marathon. You have to be able to endure adversity in order to achieve your dreams. You don't need to be the fastest. You don't need to be the smartest. You don't have to be the most qualified. You just have to be committed and have the willingness to persist. Setbacks are a part of the journey. Use them as guideposts to help you get to your destination. When you get knocked down, bounce back and find a way to win. Overcome your hardships and stick with your dreams. When you feel weak, never forget that there's strength within you. Through it all, no matter what you face, never lose your passion for living. Stay ambitious and understand that life's challenges are just an invitation for you to bring out the lion that lives within. Be unstoppable.

SOMEBODY...
SOMEWHERE...

IS COUNTING ON YOU
TO BE AT YOUR BEST...

THE HERO'S
JOURNEY

WHEN YOUR DREAMS BECOME BIGGER THAN YOU...YOU'LL FIND THE WILL TO SUCCEED

D o you think you would approach each day differently if you knew you were a hero? Would you look at yourself in a different manner or make different decisions knowing that you had "super powers", and that someone was counting on you? Here's the truth about you—*YOU ARE A HERO*. Whether you know it or not, whether you believe it or not, whether it looks like it now or not—*YOU ARE A HERO*. It doesn't matter what anybody else has said to you, has said you were or were not, you have within you the ability to be a hero in your life and you can be a hero in the lives of others. It's when you take your own heroic journey that you'll be able to evolve into a greater you. There's a purpose for your life that's bigger than you. In this chapter, you'll discover how living your purpose can create new horizons and help you come alive.

YOU WERE BORN TO BE A HERO?

What is a hero? They are an ordinary person who taps into their inner power and conquers obstacles. Even when the odds are stacked against them, they still overcome. They battle past their personal limitations in order to make a difference. Their vision of a better future is what fuels them to do extraordinary things. They find strength from their personal mission and are driven by their cause.

A hero is brave and actively demonstrates courage. They travel into the unknown, navigate through the uncertain, and find solutions to unanswered problems. Taking their journey one step at a time.

This journey may look different for each person, but the stages are the same. The first stage is when the hero separates from the world they're used to. The next stage is when the hero is initiated by a challenge and discovers their greater potential. The last stage is when the hero realizes their purpose, and after being reborn, renewed, and empowered by their struggle, the hero comes back to save, empower, and inspire others. In *The Dark Knight Rises,* Bruce Wayne was thrown into the prison and had to climb out of the pit to save the burning Gotham City. In *Black Panther,* T'Challa had to overcome being thrown down the waterfall to return and reclaim the throne of Wakanda. Every hero has a journey. It's through their efforts to maximize their life that they indirectly give others permission to do the same. They demonstrate to others that they too can dream, explore, and discover their own greatness—they can activate their own personal power and become a champion. Heroes return, not only to take back everything that has been lost, but more importantly, to rescue those who may be trapped in the same struggle. They become stronger than their fears, fueled by their passion, and led by their purpose...this is what makes them a hero.

Does this storyline sound familiar? It's really the story of anybody who looks to do anything worthwhile in their life. It's the story of that person who aims to live their dreams and make a difference. It's the story of anyone who wants to come alive. This is your story, but under one condition—you have to take your journey. You have to accept the responsibility of success.

WHAT IS SUCCESS?

Are you a hero because you drive the most luxurious car? Live in the most beautiful home? Are you a hero because you have a huge social media following? Or carry a high status? Not at all—there's more to being a hero than the things you accumulate in life. Being a hero is more about what you give rather than what you can get. Success is a word that is often described loosely. So many people get caught up in the cultural definition of success, the definition that society promotes—money, power, prestige, beauty, brilliance, status, your social media following, how many likes you get, or how many views you have. Many people get caught in the trap of trying to do whatever they can to measure up to what society labels as success. People post any and everything on social media in hopes to go viral. They'll do nearly anything to get the attention of others. They'll do what's popular all in hopes to fit in. Some will promote a fake life just to "*look successful*". Is this really what success is about? Not at all—in reality, success is much deeper than these surface level categories. You can have all the money in the world, but still be unsatisfied. You can have millions following you through your social platforms, but still feel lonely. You can climb the corporate ladder or have the most respected title at your job, but still be unhappy. The cultural definition of success may supply you with temporary satisfaction, but it will only last for so long. There will always seem to be something missing.

What is that something? What is that feeling we all seek? It's the same feeling that George Mallory climbed towards when he became one of the first to reach the summit of Mount Everest. It's the same feeling that Florence Chadwick swam towards when she became the first woman to swim the Catalina Channel. It's the same feeling that leaders like Nelson Mandela, Martin Luther King Jr., Mother Theresa, and Ghandi fought to experience...It's the feeling that every human being is after—fulfillment.

Fulfillment is a layer of happiness. It's the result of one living up to their potential, to take an idea and make it a reality. To work towards something that matters and bring about something you desired. It gives you a satisfaction that energizes you and it's not based on what others want for you or what society expects of you, but it's based on what you want and what you value. It's in the moments when you go beyond what you've been programmed to do and achieve something unexpected that you get a taste of fulfillment. When you are in connection with your true self and appreciate all that life has given you...that's fulfillment. When you are actively working to give life all that's within you...that's fulfillment. When you look at your life's work and realize that it's positively impacted someone...that's fulfillment. It's what you feel when you know that what you do with your life has meaning and is bigger than just you.

The beauty of fulfillment, and even of success, is that it can be different for everyone. You get to determine what success is for your life. It doesn't have to be the same as someone else's. One person's definition of success can be different from another's. Differences are what make the world such a wonderful place. We're not supposed to be the same. If we were, how boring would life be? We have each been born into our own uniqueness, which gives us access to our own experience in life.

Whether you're the CEO of a company or the janitor that maintains the facility, you can be fulfilled. Whether you're a movie star on the big screen or a missionary helping to combat poverty, you can be fulfilled. Every hero has something that brings him or her fulfillment. Success begins with determining what it is that you value and making what you value your life's work.

I've grown to define success as loving yourself, loving what you do, and loving how you do it. I believe that this is a great recipe for living my greatest life—being able to look myself in the mirror and say that I love the person I am becoming. Waking up every day with passion, enjoying how I spend my time, and constantly improving as a person, is what I aim for. Viewing success from this perspective sends me on a never-ending journey of becoming my best, and when you are at your best, you'll inspire those around you to be at their best. This philosophy helps me make decisions and structure my life. You don't have to subscribe to this definition. I'm just illustrating how when you get clear on what success means to you, your approach to life will be influenced by your philosophy. Your attitude, your decisions, and your environment, will all be influenced by your definition of and commitment to success.

Create your own standard and live your life based on what you value. You can find enjoyment in what you choose to do with your life if you give what you do meaning.

THE ULTIMATE SOURCE

There is one question that every human being wishes to answer. It's summed up in this Mark Twain quote, *"The two most important days in your life are the day you are born and the day you find out why"*. Why were you born? What is the meaning behind your life? This is a question that we all should contemplate—because when you realize the value that you offer to the world your life changes forever.

Whether you know it or not, your life has purpose. There is meaning behind your existence. It's not by accident that you are alive. It's not a coincidence that you were born. You are no mistake. You have been placed on this earth for a specific reason. Regardless of what anybody has ever said about you or in spite of the things that you've experienced, you were created for such a time as this and there's something within you that will add value to others.

Here's how wonderfully you've been designed and created—at the time of this writing there are nearly 7 billion people that are currently living on earth, and not one of them have the same finger print as you. Out of all the people who have lived before you, and those who will be born after you, not one of them has shared or will share your fingerprint. Your fingerprint is unique to you. It's special to you, demonstrating that you have been born to leave a print on this world that only you can make. Just being born is a true miracle in itself. Scientists have estimated that the odds of each of us being born are nearly 1 in 400 trillion.

You are a miracle and we each have to start living like the miracles that we are. You are fearfully and wonderfully made. Your race, culture, traits, and personality have all been crafted to make you who you are. You don't have to waste your time trying to be someone else, because there's something special about your uniqueness. There is a purpose as to why you are alive. Embrace that reason and fulfill it. When you live your life on purpose, you'll become that hero.

You don't have to wait to be told by anyone that you are great. The richest experiences in our lives aren't when we're searching for validation from others, but when we're listening to our own inner voice, doing something that matters, doing it well, and doing it in the service of a cause that is larger than ourselves. Our best moments usually come when our body and mind are stretched to their limits in a voluntary effort to accomplish something worthwhile and purposeful. We are able to thrive when we work towards something that adds value. The most successful people often aren't directly pursuing the cultural definition of success. They're working hard and persisting through difficulties because they have an internal desire to live life on their own terms, learn about their world, and accomplish something that endures and benefits those around them.

High achievers are led by purpose. Steve Jobs wanted to advance the world with the iPhone. Princess Diana became the voice for the poor and disenfranchised. Those people that press towards an objective that is greater than themselves are typically the most motivated and driven people, and usually spark something that helps change the world. Life is better lived when you find a way to connect with others and use your talents, skills, and abilities to contribute to the larger whole. You come alive when you make your goals bigger than you. Being purpose-driven will shift your focus. You'll find yourself taking a different view on your challenges, realizing that if life has a purpose, then there surely is meaning in your struggles. It's really not about what you expect from life, but it's more about what life expects from you. It's not just about what you want out of life, it's more about what life wants out of you. When you find what's within you, it's your responsibility to use it to better your world. There's strength to be found in purpose. In the worst of times, you'll be able to realize that whatever you go through, or whatever you face, can be used to benefit you. When you find yourself feeling hopeless and expecting nothing else from life, remember, the fact that your heart is still beating is proof that life is still expecting something from you. In the words of Viktor Frankl, *"The man who becomes conscious of the responsibility he bears toward a human being who affectionately waits for him, or to an unfinished work, will never be able to throw away his life."* Don't throw away your life. Come alive and leave your mark.

I spent so much time running away from myself. I didn't think that I was capable of doing anything worthwhile. Fear wanted to silence my voice, but when I developed a desire for more in my life, I started to question fear. When I started understanding the purpose behind my voice, I began to conquer fear. I began to notice how my messages would impact others, and how my words could inspire others to take on their own path of pursuing their dreams. Sometimes in life, it's the thing that scares you the most that ends up being the very thing that you are supposed to be doing. What you run away from can actually be the thing that sets you free. When I did what scared me, I quickly began to notice the bigger purpose that was behind me sharing my gifts with the world…and then something happened that made me realize just how important it is to live with a purpose and helped me understand the true magnitude of my mission.

February 11, 2015

I was in my office doing some studying when my phone started vibrating. It was my mother calling me. I picked up the phone and I could tell that something wasn't right. I could sense by her voice that what she was about to say wasn't going to be something I really wanted to hear. At the time, my grandmother had suffered a number of strokes and her health was on the decline. We had just celebrated her birthday a few days before...I started to brace myself for the news that I was about to receive. It's one thing to try to prepare for the expected, but it's another thing to get hit with the unexpected, because what my mother was about to share with me wasn't about my grandmother. She shared with me that my cousin, Ross, had been found unresponsive and he was no longer living.

After hanging up the phone I had so many questions. I couldn't believe it. It seemed unreal. I grew up having close relationships with all of my cousins. My grandmother saw to it that we all spent time together and that we would have relationships with one another. Ross was one of my younger cousins, however, he was more like a younger brother because of how close we were. I couldn't wrap my mind around the reality that he was gone.

His passing was a tough loss. We took it hard as a family. His parents were faced with something that no parent ever wants to experience—burying their child. Ross was 19 years old, and like many teenagers, was trying to find himself. A night out with friends turned into a fatal encounter when he overdosed. It was a tough reality to digest, but I don't believe God makes any mistakes. His passing opened my eyes even more to the challenges that many people face on a daily basis. In our society, people are very quick to condemn a person for their addiction and treat them like criminals, but there is a cause and a reason why someone is addicted to something—some hurt they're trying to run away from, some trauma they're trying to avoid, a void in their life or a past experience they're fighting to escape. Everybody is challenged in one way or another. There are many people fighting silent battles that no one knows about. They wrestle with hurt, they smother in depression, and they drown in pain. They haven't quite figured out the proper way to cope with their challenges, so they turn to destructive things. The road of destruction will lead you to the avenue of death, and death can wear many faces—losing your career, your relationship, your livelihood, your family, your joy, your happiness, your sanity, and in many cases even your life. Addiction, fear, anxiety, depression, suicide...these words describe dark places where many people find themselves. Some of these people you may come in contact with every single day. You work with them, do business with them, go to school with them, see them at the barbershop or the beauty salon, go to church with them, pass them at the grocery store, sit next to them at the game. Everybody is going through something, which signals the importance of us all working towards being a light in someone's darkness. We each have to take on the responsibility of delivering hope and inspiration with our unique abilities in order to make this world a better and brighter place.

There's more to life than just achieving goals. It's bigger than you simply accomplishing success, it's more about figuring out how you can help contribute to the world—helping to solve the problems that others face daily. Using your gifts to inspire and creating a chain reaction of inspiration that compels others to live their best lives, become all that they can be, make a difference, and become the hero that's within them.

After the passing of my cousin, I realized on a greater scale how important it is to do what I can with what I have to make a difference in this world and in the lives of others. His untimely death helped me gain a new perspective and a new level of drive—to help others know who they are, to think big, and to pursue the dreams that make them come alive. This has become a part of my 'Why'. Knowing that I can help and empower others to live their dreams and overcome their challenges. When I face challenges or get discouraged, I remind myself that I can't give up when someone needs what I have to offer. Knowing that I can help change lives is what fuels me. It keeps me pushing when the journey towards success gets hard. There's so much power in having a 'why'.

YOUR WHY

Who is waiting for you to be at your best? Who's waiting to be inspired by seeing you operate in your gifts? Who's waiting to be empowered by your story? The truth is that you have to go all in on your dream, because someone is waiting and counting on you to come alive.

The first step in figuring out how you're going to achieve your dream is to understand why it's important. Entrepreneur, Jim Rohn once said, "*The bigger the 'why' the easier the how.*" Your 'why', will have you tapping into reserves of energy, determination, and courage that you never even knew you had. Knowing your why' will help you focus your efforts on what matters most and will compel you to move your mission forward and take risks regardless of the obstacles that may stand in front of you. It's when you know your 'why' that you'll find yourself motivated to move into a more challenging but fulfilling path in life.

Your 'why' keeps your mission clear and your goal compelling. When you feel like giving up...remember why you started. When you don't feel like putting in the work...remember why it's important. There will be times when your dreams will seem impossible, but knowing your 'why' will influence you to find a way to make things work. You find strength when you remember that your family is counting on you. You find courage when you realize your community is waiting on you. You find confidence when you realize there are others that believe in you. Passion isn't just found in what you do, it's found in why you do it. What are you living for? What mark do you want to leave? What do you want to be remembered for?

One of the deep human desires that often influences our lives and daily decisions is the search for meaning. We each want to know that we matter, that we hold value, and that our life has significance. There have been many topics related to personal achievement discussed throughout this book, but, if you were only to take one thought with you, take this...YOU MATTER. You count. You do make a difference. It's your duty to shine your light, and when you do, you'll experience happiness and a joy in life that is immeasurable.

Become the hero that you were created to be. Don't be the hero who never takes his journey. Don't be intimidated by your purpose, be fueled by your 'why'. There's something within you that can and will add value to others. There's someone waiting to benefit from what's inside of you. Let it out. Unleash it. Give it permission to live. Nothing can stop a man on a mission to accomplish something that has a purpose that's bigger than him. So realize that your dreams are bigger than you. No matter what you may face, no matter what stands in your way, allow your purpose and your 'why' to bring out the greatness that you have within. Come alive.

CONCLUSION

DO MORE OF WHAT
MAKES YOU COME ALIVE

W*hat makes you come alive?* Whatever it is…make it your mission to go after it. The greatest adventure that you can ever take on is to live the life of your dreams. You may think that you're not ready, you're incapable, or that now is not the right time, but I hope by now you realize that you have the freedom to change your life at any instant. You get to decide and determine who you will be in each moment of your life.

Let the next moment of your life be where you become more of who you truly are.

Disconnect from the lies and the deceptions that my be corrupting your identity and connect with more of your truth.

Think big…and then dream bigger. Never putting any limits on what's possible.

Believe in yourself and never lose hope in the possibility of your dreams.

Don't let what may be going on around you effect what's happening within you. Speak the language of possibility…

I CAN. I WILL. MY DREAMS ARE POSSIBLE.

Decide who you want to be, what you want to do, and where you want to take your life…and stick with your vision. Become one with it and don't allow anything or anybody to take it away from you.

The road will get difficult and struggles will arise, but remember that you were given this life because you are strong enough to live it.

You may not have control over everything that happens but you always have control over how you respond. With everything that you face, life will give you a chance to respond. A response is just another opportunity for you to control your destiny. Not allowing situations and circumstances to determine your fate, but making the decision to turn misfortune into profit, pain into power, struggle into success. Respond with your vision, your purpose, and your goals in mind.

When I was laid of and told, "*I was no longer needed...*" My response became that someone else needed me. Others were waiting to witness my gifts. I was given the opportunity to control my destiny and I pursued my dream.

You too have the freedom to build the life that you envision.

Be better than your best yesterday. To get all you want you have to give all you have. Maximum effort produces maximum success. Great effort produces a great reward. You can always get better. Strive for greatness and live with excellence. Make growth apart of your lifestyle.

In the days when you question yourself and feel like you're not built for your dream...remember, you're built for whatever you're willing to fight for.

You won't have all the answers. You won't have everything figured out...but have faith, desire, and keep fighting for your vision. Because if you trust yourself now, you'll thank yourself later.

You'll get knocked down, you'll get told "NO" and it may seem like you're being undervalued and overlooked....but keep fighting for your success.

You will come face to face with failure, hit by the unexpected, and blindsided by disappointments...but keep fighting for your dreams.

No matter what you face as you take your journey towards your calling, choose to be unstoppable because the one that never gives up is the one that wins.

What lives inside of you is the best-kept secret that the world needs. Give the world something it didn't know it was missing. It's not a matter of what you could do or should do...it's a matter of what you must do, what you need to do.

You've been placed on this earth to do things that only you can do. It's really not you that's chasing after your dreams...your dreams are chasing after you. Don't run away from what's calling you.

Be all that you were intended to be. Take the risk of going too far...because it's only then that you'll be able to find out how far you can go.

...And when you've reached the point that you feel like you can go on, remember somebody somewhere is counting on you to be at your best. In the words of the great philosopher, Howard Thurman, "*Don't ask yourself what the world needs. Ask yourself what makes you come alive, and go do that, because what the world needs is people who have come alive.*"

Be POWERFUL!

David
Gibson

STAY CONNECTED

For resources related to this book and more personal development tools:
Visit www.elevationisamust.com

For daily inspiration and insights on achieving your
goals be sure to stay connected on social media:

@D1GIBSON

@D1GIBSON

@D1GIBSON

/DAVIDGIBSON

ACKNOWLEDGMENTS

A special thank you to my amazing wife Amanda, our son Trip, and my parents David Sr. and Verlinda, who each have inspired me in so many ways to strive to be a better me. To my late grandmothers, Onia and Memaw, the wisdom that you both instilled in me is timeless and I am forever grateful for the blessing of being able to share moments with the two of you. To all who have poured into me and saw greater for me even during the times when I didn't see greater for myself...Thank you! To my amazing #DreamCatchers Worldwide Community...Thank you all for your support and encouragement as we collectively work to inspire the world...and to YOU, thank you for taking time out to come into my world and discover what it means to me to COME ALIVE. My hopes are that something in this book will lead you to take action. Take action on overcoming challenges. Take action on living your purpose. Take action on unleashing the real you.
COME ALIVE...

Made in the USA
Monee, IL
04 September 2019